the good-carb
diet for life

linda gassenheimer

kyle books

the good-carb
diet for life

By the author of *Good-Carb Meals in Minutes*

linda gassenheimer

kyle books

**To Harold for his love of good food and his
enthusiastic support for this project.**

This edition published in 2005 by Kyle Books
An imprint of Kyle Cathie Limited
general.enquiries@kyle-cathie.com
www.kylecathie.com

Distributed by National Book Network
4501 Forbes Blvd., Suite 200
Lanham, MD 20706
Phone: (301) 459 3366 Fax: (301) 429 5746

ISBN 1 904920 26 8

Text © 2003 Linda Gassenheimer

Special Photography and Styling: Juliet Piddington
Home Economy: Carol Tennant
Production: Lorraine Baird and Sha Huxtable

Linda Gassenheimer is hereby identified as the author of this work
in accordance with Section 77 of the Copyright, Designs and Patents Act
1988.

The Library of Congress Cataloguing-in-Publication Data is available on file.

Color separations by Scanhouse
Printed and bound by Rose Printing Company, Inc.

contents

foreword

Over the past decade there have been more questions than answers about whether carbohydrates are good or evil. Some diets push carbohydrates while others totally eliminate them. Finally, results of recent nutrition research on a common hormone condition, insulin resistance, offers the right answer for many. This condition affects almost half of all Americans and an even higher percent of those who are overweight.

Inherited as a survival gene, insulin resistance provided a way for our hunter/gatherer ancestors to efficiently store fat and survive a famine. People with insulin resistance produce higher-than-normal amounts of insulin after eating carbohydrates. This promotes an increase in fat storing. Modern-day food manufacturing technology and the rarity of famines in Western culture have resulted in an overabundance of low-cost, good-tasting, super-refined starchy and sugary foods. Our ancient genetic hardwiring has not been able to keep up with cultural modernization. As a result, insulin resistance is now the root cause of our "lifestyle diseases," replacing its previous role in promoting survival.

Eating carbohydrates in excess causes repeated demands for more and more insulin. High insulin levels accelerate obesity. This phenomenon explains the obesity pandemic threatening both adults and children in this country. Abnormally high insulin levels also cause serious detriments to every organ of the body. Insulin resistance promotes heart attacks and strokes because it causes high blood pressure, abnormal cholesterol levels, atherosclerosis, and blood clotting disorders. Insulin resistance precedes every case of adult-onset diabetes. Polycystic ovarian syndrome (PCOS), the most common cause of female infertility and hormone dysfunction, is now recognized as originating from insulin resistance.

The National Institute of Health (NIH) have cited insulin resistance as the "epidemic of the modern era." Unfortunately, most people don't know they have insulin resistance. The NIH has issued a plea to health professionals to aggressively screen for it. The condition is very easy to treat and all the associated disease processes can be eliminated. The treatment starts with modifying our American diet.

If carbohydrates aggravate insulin resistance, then wouldn't the solution be to eliminate all carbohydrates? Indeed, severe carbohydrate restriction has been the dieting hype this past decade. Besides being totally unrealistic, impractical, and a proven disaster for long-term weight loss, carbohydrate deprivation is also not without its cost to health. Inadequate carbohydrate intake leads to depression, fatigue, mood instability, and sleep disturbances.

My medical experience in treating 5,000 weight-loss patients over the past seven years (almost all of whom had insulin resistance) has proven that eating carbohydrates is not only possible but is recommended to maintain proper physical and mental health. The key to properly eating carbohydrates is in knowing which kinds and amounts can be comfortably tolerated without causing an abnormal insulin response.

Linda's *Good-Carb* books have been a valuable resource for my patients. Her nutritional information aligns with our medical philosophy about insulin resistance. I commend her efforts to include all the food groups—protein, carbohydrates, and fats—in all her menu formats. Her consistent simplicity in food preparation is especially appreciated. No treatment is more doomed than expecting someone to follow a complicated, restrictive, elaborate, time-consuming dietary regimen.

Her shopping lists provide the detail necessary to improve efficiency and her menu plans help eliminate unnecessary guesswork. I find her recipe format with nutritional value listings extremely helpful, especially the unusual but important information on saturated fat and fiber content.

An especially wonderful feature of Linda's books is her gourmet recipes for entertaining. The freedom of creating and serving one of Linda's culinary feasts completely eliminates the social isolation often felt during dieting. It's hard to believe the recipes are so healthy. I actually write prescriptions for my patients to get these books. Linda's *Good-Carb Meals in Minutes* and *Good-Carb Diet for Life* are consistent with my medical philosophy about what food should be: simple, snappy, scientifically sound, and scrumptious.

Good-Carb Diet for Life is a successful blend of healthful dining and gastronomic gusto—simply, one of life's great pleasures. Enjoy.

A Salute To Your Health

Cheryle R. Hart, M.D.

Author of *The Insulin Resistance Diet*

introduction

Nine years ago my husband came home from a visit to the cardiologist and said, "My doctor wants me to reduce my carbohydrate intake." His triglycerides were high and climbing and he was having trouble losing the few pounds he had gained on holiday. This was a new challenge for me. I didn't want to follow the route of gimmick eating: no eating all the eggs and bacon you want or eating at certain times of the day or with certain food combinations. On the other hand, as I watched him struggle to put together reduced carb meals, I realized that this was going to be a challenge for both of us. Bagels for breakfast and cans of sugary soft drinks after tennis were out. And what could he substitute for crackers and potato chips with drinks? I wanted a real eating lifestyle that fitted our busy lives, our eating out, entertaining. Most of all I wanted good food that was good for us, too.

I worked with two cardiologists, an endocrinologist, and nutritionists to create an eating lifestyle that was healthy and balanced. What I found was that the doctors and nutritionists could readily explain why this approach worked, but could not tell me how to adapt it to my busy life. In fact, when I attended medical lectures with these doctors, the reception for the diet was highly enthusiastic, but the questions at the end were, "How do I do it? What do I eat?" The recipes I created had to be lower in carbohydrates, use lean proteins and mono-unsaturated fats (olive and canola oil), and most of all be delicious. The result was my book, *Good-Carb Meals in Minutes*, which was so well received it reached number one on Amazon.com's bestseller list. What prompted me to write this sequel was the incredible response from readers:

"Your cookbook *Good-Carb Meals in Minutes* was truly an inspiration to me, and I attribute most of my weight loss of 30lb to using your healthy and delicious recipes (husband pleasers as well)."

"I just want to let you know how well-organized the cookbook is, and how tasty all of the recipes are. I am still in the Quick Start phase of the book, but have found that the recipes are so varied. I see it more as a change in my diet, rather than being 'on' a diet. The way your meals are set up forces me to plan things out, and not resort to 'quick' fixes. Thanks again for putting together a great cookbook!"

"So many of your menus are part of my daily repertoire now. I have tried to plan good-carb meals for three years but with a full-time job and other obligations, I found that what my husband and I were eating was boring. I know what to do and how to do it but it takes time—you have done all the planning and all I have to do after a day's work is to drop in to the supermarket and I can have a good tasting meal in half an hour or less! What I have enjoyed most are the sauces that accompany the poultry or fish, which deliver great flavor."

"Our particular favorite is the chocolate soufflé dessert. It is hard for me to believe that something so delicious is not bad for you."

"My husband has high blood pressure and high cholesterol and we are looking for a good diet to follow. This one is the right ticket. Have tried the recipes and love them."

Good-Carb Meals in Minutes is a three-step program to losing weight and keeping it off. The first, Quick Start, is a two-week menu that jump-starts quick weight loss. Which Carbs is the next two-week step that gradually reintroduces carbohydrates into the menu while you are still losing weight. The final phase, Right Carbs, is a balanced menu that shows you how to eat the right carbohydrates and keep the weight off. *Good-Carb Diet for Life* gives an entirely new two weeks of meals for each of these phases.

A new feature in this book is a Super Speed Supper section containing even quicker dinners for busy week nights, based on buying partially prepared ingredients from the supermarket. The supermarkets have come a long way in helping us get our meals on the table in minutes. For those nights when you want to get dinner ready in 15 minutes, this section has meals that can be quickly assembled into a good-carb meal at home.

Another feature is a Weekends section containing meals that are a little special when you have some extra time. You can enjoy the weekend and not feel that dreaded Monday morning I-have-to-be-good syndrome.

I have, also, answered the question of how to entertain within the eating lifestyle with five different party menus that won't break the carb or calorie scale. I had some friends over for dinner and they phoned the next day to say how much they loved the food but were afraid to get on the scales after having seconds. I told them to forget the scales. All of the foods fit the good-carb guidelines, and they didn't have to worry. The Entertaining section here is filled with this style of food. From football parties to a casual dinner with friends to an elegant dinner for eight, you can choose whichever menu suits your needs. The parties in this section use ingredients that can be bought in one-stop shopping at the local supermarket. The recipes take minutes to make and many can be made ahead. I give you a shopping list and countdown explaining how far in advance the recipe can be made, how to store it, and how to reheat and serve it.

While producing my radio program in Miami, I was surprised that several of the men at the radio station were trying to cut back on their carbohydrates. Their first questions were, "What's on the list?" and "What's off the list?" I myself was lost when I first tried to make good-carbohydrate meals. I had to fundamentally rethink my approach and I started by restocking the pantry and refrigerator. The changes were dramatic.

Off the list were

- Low-fat processed foods such as fat-free cookies and cakes, and other sugary desserts
- Fat-free mayonnaise, salad dressings, cream cheese, and sour cream
- Condiments, sauces, and salsas where sugar is one of the first five ingredients
- Pancakes, bagels, and waffles
- Jams and jellies
- Pizza and platefuls of pasta as a main course
- Garnished baked potato as a meal
- Sugary soft drinks and fruit juices
- Chips, pretzels, and popcorn

On the list were

- Eggs, as many as four a week (We hadn't eaten them for breakfast in 10 years.)
- Egg substitute (which is basically egg whites), as a good source of protein

- A well-stocked vegetable drawer, including cucumbers, lettuce, celery, bell peppers, mushrooms, and tomatoes
- Lean deli meats, such as turkey breast, chicken, ham, and roast beef
- Brown rice and whole wheat pasta, in place of the lower fiber, less nutritious white varieties
- High-fiber, wholegrain breads that are relatively low in carbs
- No-sugar-added tomato sauce and salad dressings
- Real mayonnaise made with soybean or olive oil
- High-fiber, no-sugar-added bran cereal for breakfast
- Olive and canola oil
- Walnuts, pecans, almonds, and peanuts
- Eight glasses (3 pints) of water per day

With this list of dos and don'ts, my husband lost weight, has kept it off for seven years, and lowered his blood cholesterol and triglyceride counts to healthy levels.

Millions of people are now giving up their sandwiches and pasta meals as after unsuccessful attempts at weight loss from low-fat, high-carb diets, they're finally getting the results they want from a good-carb lifestyle. The theory behind good-carbohydrate diets is this: eating lots of carbohydrates over-stimulates insulin production, causing peaks and valleys in blood sugar levels that, in turn, create hunger pangs. On the other hand, protein is digested more slowly, promoting more even blood sugar levels. Eating more protein, fewer carbs, and more mono-unsaturated fat promotes weight loss by decreasing fat storage, increasing fat burning, and delaying the onset of hunger pangs.

Several cardiologists steered me away from diets that call for high levels of saturated fat. The menus in this book are similar to a Mediterranean-style diet using fresh vegetables, mono-unsaturated olive, and canola oils, and lean meats and fish.

These meals follow the same guidelines as in Good-Carb Meals in Minutes: attractive, delicious, fun, healthy, complete meals that are quick and easy to make. All the breakfast, lunch, and dinner menus are presented as entire meals, so you don't have to think about how to cook a dish or what goes with what.

I developed these techniques after many years of juggling my family, career, and a desire for good food.

My *Dinner in Minutes* newspaper columns have simple, easy-to-follow recipes. From years of training, I've learned to use classic techniques and familiar combinations to produce delicious results while cutting the cooking time. It's a blueprint that can be used for everyday meals or dressed up for parties or special occasions.

Special Features

Shopping List

The Good-Carb Diet for Life blueprint contains a shopping list based on how the food is bought in the shops.

- Quick shopping is as important as quick cooking. You won't have to think about how many mushrooms to buy. I've given you the amount.
- I list the ingredients by supermarket aisles to help you navigate with ease.
- I've included tips on how to get in and out of the supermarket fast and how to take advantage of today's timesaving prepared foods.
- The shopping list saves you both time and money since you buy only what you need.
- The staples list helps you organize your store cupboards so that they are not filled with

extraneous items. To help you plan your pantry, I have included a separate section using the staples listed in the book. You will already have many of the ingredients for the recipes and only need to buy a few fresh items.

Shopping Guidelines

Many of the recipes call for prepared condiments such as salad dressings, pasta sauce, and Chinese sauces.

- To help you pick the brands that will fit the nutritional guidelines, I have added a section that tells you what to look for on the nutritional labels of the products.
- Keep the products that you like best on hand.

Helpful Hints and Countdown

Each meal contains helpful hints on shopping, cooking, and substitutions, as well as a countdown so you can get the whole meal on the table at the same time.

- You can hit the kitchen on the run without having to plan or think about each step.
- In my home, the dinner preparation encompasses the time I turn on the light in the kitchen until the plates are brought to the table.
- The helpful hints tell you what to buy, how to

buy, and what you can substitute. They include tips on the best preparation method and quick-cooking techniques, as well as timesaving clean-up tips.

● *The Good-Carb Diet for Life* doesn't mean broiled chicken every night. You will find a variety of delicious meals covering many ethnic flavors.

● As you eat your way through this book, you can enjoy Tuscan Chicken; Five-Spice Tuna Tataki; Whisky-Soused Salmon; Mahi Mahi Satay with Thai Peanut Sauce; and Mexican Sopes. Wherever I travel throughout the world, I go to street markets with chefs, taste their foods, and bring back their flavors to add to the repertoire of simple, good-carb recipes.

Flexibility

A blueprint means that it is totally flexible.

● When you choose a fish recipe, you can buy the freshest-looking fish in the shop rather than the fish called for in the recipe.

● You can use the best sirloin or fillet steak, or more economical cuts like flank and skirt steaks.

● All of the recipes were tested to produce delicious results with products obtained by one-stop shopping in your local supermarket.

● Branching out to use the freshest and best

ingredients, like an infused olive oil or aged balsamic vinegar, will add even more zip to these recipes.

● You can use the ingredients called for or change them within the blueprint to suit your taste.

● This flexible approach lets you choose whatever is in season, on sale, or just fits your mood.

As I mentioned above, this good-carbohydrate lifestyle is divided into three phases: an initial phase of significant carbohydrate reduction, an intermediate phase for reintroduction of carbs, and a maintenance phase of balanced eating.

QUICK START—The first step to a successful eating plan calls for a reduction of carbohydrates. While differences exist, most proponents advise a level of about 30–40 grams of carbs a day. My Quick Start section maintains that level through healthy recipes containing vegetables and lean proteins.

WHICH CARBS—Carbohydrates are an important nutrient and the second step reintroduces high-fiber, low-simple-sugar carbohydrates at a level permitting continued weight loss. Listening to the questions from the participants in my good-carb classes, I realized the second phase is the most difficult. They are afraid that returning to higher levels of carbohydrates will negate all of the benefits they've achieved.

RIGHT CARBS—The third stage leaves you permanently with the Right Carbs to maintain your weight loss. This section achieves a well-balanced lifestyle of approximately 40 percent calories from carbohydrates, 30 percent calories from lean proteins, and 30 percent calories from fat (primarily mono-unsaturated).

So how does my husband handle holidays and blow-out weekends? Remember, balance is the key. We have found that you can splurge on special occasions without negative effects when you come back to the Right Carbs. In fact, one cardiologist adviser said that varying from a good base once in a while still leaves you much better off than if you don't have that base at all. In other words, the good-carbohydrate approach is forgiving. My husband found that returning to the Right Carbs is easy because it takes so little effort and any time you want to restart weight loss, you can go back to Quick Start for a week or two and work yourself back up to Right Carbs. My husband and I no longer think about what is and isn't good-carb—we just consider it good food that fits into his busy schedule.

Before you start a program of this type, it is always best to check with your doctor first. This is especially true if you are taking any medication under a doctor's care. If your doctor recommends a blood test, it will provide a baseline against which to compare your results.

My goal in sharing these recipes with you is to help you enjoy good food for good health. My husband and I love good food. Now, with these recipes, we can live to eat and eat to live. We hope you enjoy them too. Bon appétit.

Smart Shopping the Good-Carb Way

Here are some tips that will help get you in and out of the shops quickly. It should help you with the I-hate-to-shop syndrome.

Some Advice

The adage of "Don't go shopping on an empty stomach" is true. It can be a disaster. If I go to the shops when I'm tired and hungry, I just get to a starving point and eat anything offered to me. However, if you have a snack before you go, you will concentrate on what you should be buying instead of what you shouldn't buy.

Try to go to the supermarket when it isn't crowded or directly after you've put in a long day's work. Carry a cooler in your car so you can stop on the way to work, during lunch, or at other times. (The cooler will protect foods from moderate heat and cold. It won't help with extreme heat or freezing temperatures.)

Keep the foods from my staples list on hand. (See page 19.) You will only need to pick up a few fresh items to complete your meal.

Supermarket Savvy

Let the Markets Help You

Supermarkets are constantly updating their product mix to help us get our meals on the table fast. Use the supermarket to your advantage.

Salad Bars

These are great for picking up a quick salad or lunch or buying cut vegetables and fruits for cooking at home.

Deli

Look for new leaner cuts of cooked meats—all with nutritional analysis. Ham and roast beef have been made leaner and without high carbs.

Dairy

Reduced-fat cheese has come a long way. Gone is the rubbery cheese that won't melt. Many brands using new techniques have developed lower-fat cheeses with flavor and that melt well.

Prepared Foods

Ask for roast chicken breast only. Ask for an ingredients list. Read the labels carefully for all prepared foods. Many have added salt and sugar. Many prepared sauces and condiments are now made in a low-salt, reduced carbohydrate version. Look for these in the supermarket. (See page 12 for Shopping Guidelines.)

Fruit and Veg Department

Bags of washed, ready-to-eat salads have been one of the best conveniences I've seen. Read the labels. If they don't say ready-to-eat or washed, then you will need to wash the ingredients prior to using.

Shredded carrots, lettuce, and coleslaw mixtures are another big help in getting meals on the table in minutes.

Many supermarkets have cubes of melons and pineapple ready to eat.

Meat Department

Look for lower fat or lean meats. Many stores now have separate sections for lean meats or mark them with special labels.

There are many marinated or pre-cooked meats available. Watch for sugar, salt, and fat content.

Roasted chicken breast, strips, and pieces are available. The ones without skin or honey sauces are perfect for salads, sandwiches, and soups.

Grocery Aisles

There are many items that make our lives easier and more are coming out each day. Low-fat, no-sugar-added tomato sauce, pasta sauces, and salad dressings are a few of the products. In fact, there are so many available, it's best to try a few and, when you find one you like, keep a few bottles on hand. Most important is to read the nutritional labels and ingredients lists. (See page 17 for the Shopping Guidelines.)

How to Read the Labels

When you're shopping, it's worth a few extra minutes to read the food labels. They can be confusing. Here are some answers to the most frequently asked questions.

What do "reduced fat," "low fat," and "light" mean?

"Low fat" means 3 grams of fat or fewer per serving. "Reduced fat" means at least 25 percent less fat per serving than the regular version of the same food. "Sugar free," according to the FDA, must contain fewer than 0.5 gram per serving. "Light" generally means that the food contains 50 percent fewer calories from fat than the regular version of the same food.

Check the serving size on the label. It can be misleading. If the serving size is 1 tablespoon, you need to think if that is the amount you will actually eat.

Ingredients must be listed in descending order by weight. Generally, if an ingredient is fifth or lower in the list, it has minimal amounts in each serving.

Shopping Guidelines

Throughout the book I use prepared products from the supermarket. There are many brands that will fit the bill but there is considerable variation in their content. The best advice is to find the product that fits the nutritional analysis and has the best flavor. Once you've found one you prefer, keep it on hand.

Here are some guidelines on what to look for on nutritional labels:

Oil and Vinegar Dressing, Balsamic Dressing, Vinaigrettes

The nutritional analysis for meals using one of these ingredients is based on olive oil or canola oil dressings. Try to stay away from nonfat dressings. In general when they cut the fat, they add carbohydrates.

Quantity	Calories	Carbohydrates
1 tablespoon	75	0.5–1.5g

Mayonnaise

soybean oil, canola oil, or olive oil (Major brands are made with soybean oil.)

Quantity	Calories	Carbohydrates
1 tablespoon	100	0g

Reduced Fat Mayonnaise

Quantity	Calories	Carbohydrates	Fat
1 tablespoon	50	1g	5g

Caesar Dressing

Quantity	Calories	Carbohydrates
1 tablespoon	80	0.5–1.5g

Tomato and Pasta Sauces

Look for no-sugar-added, no-salt-added, or low-sodium brands. There are many excellent ones to choose from.

Quantity	Calories	Carbohydrates	Fiber	Sodium	Fat
1 cup	60–80	12–14g	2–3g	40mg	0g

Nonfat, Low-Sodium Chicken Broth

Quantity	Calories	Sodium
1 cup	15	560mg

Low-Sodium Soy Sauce

Quantity	Calories	Sodium
1 tablespoon	10	574mg

Tortilla

Quantity	Calories	Carbohydrates
6 inch tortilla weighing	90	16g

Whole Wheat Bread

Quantity	Calories	Carbohydrates	Fiber
1 slice	50	10g	3g

Other Breads and Rolls

Quantity	Calories	Carbohydrates	Fiber
1 slice/1 roll	80	15g	0.7–2g

Cereal: Fiber One*

Quantity	Calories	Carbohydrates	Fiber
1 ounce	80	24g	13g

Cereal: All-Bran and Bran Buds*

Quantity	Calories	Carbohydrates	Fiber
1/2 cup	80	24g	13g

* For cereals: Read labels carefully; labels say they're healthy, but you need to look for the amounts of sugar, molasses, corn syrup, or honey

For an Ham and Canadian Bacon

Quantity	Calories	Sodium	Fat
1 ounce	37	246mg	1.4g

Reduced-Fat, Part Skim Milk Mozzarella Cheese

Quantity	Calories	Fat	Sodium
1 ounce	72	4.5g	132mg

Pimientos

Quantity	Calories	Carbohydrates	Fat	Sodium
1 cup	40	8g	0g	20mg

Marinated Artichoke Hearts

Quantity	Calories	Carbohydrates	Fat	Sodium
1 ounce	25	2g	1.5g	90mg

Unsweetened Applesauce

Quantity	Calories	Carbohydrate	Sodium
1 cup	100	30g	30mg

Low-Fat Frozen Yogurt

Quantity	Calories	Fat	Carbohydrates
1/2 cup	120	3g	20g

Staples

This is a comprehensive list of the staples listed in the recipes. Keep these staples on hand and you'll only need to pick up a few fresh items to make quick meals.

Canned or Bottled Goods

Dijon mustard

Fat-free, low-salt chicken broth

Low-sodium tomato or V-8 juice

Low-sodium, no-sugar-added tomato sauce and diced tomatoes

Mayonnaise made with olive or soybean oil

No-sugar-added olive oil and vinegar dressing

No-sugar-added tomato salsa

Reduced-fat mayonnaise

Canned chickpeas, black beans, navy beans, cannellini (white kidney) beans, red kidney beans

Canned tuna packed in water

Condiments

Hot pepper sauce

Low-sodium soy sauce

Worcestershire sauce

Dairy

Butter

Egg substitute

Eggs

Light yogurt

Parmesan cheese

Skim milk

Dry Goods

Cornstarch

High-fiber, no-sugar-added bran cereal

Oatmeal

Salt

Sugar substitute

Whole wheat flour

Whole wheat pasta

Freezer Goods

Frozen chopped onion

Frozen diced green bell pepper

Grains and Breads

Brown rice (30-minute quick-cooking and 10-minute quick-cooking)

100% whole wheat bread

Lentils

Multigrain bread

Rye bread

Whole wheat pitta bread

Whole wheat tortilla

Wild rice

Oils and Vinegars

Balsamic vinegar

Distilled white vinegar

Olive oil

Olive oil spray

Canola oil

Red wine vinegar

Rice vinegar

Produce Department

Carrots

Celery

Garlic

Lemon

Red onions

Yellow onions

Spices and Herbs

Black peppercorns

Cayenne pepper

Chili powder

Dried chopped sage

Dried dill

Dried oregano

Dried rosemary

Dried tarragon

Dried thyme

Freeze-dried chives

Grated nutmeg

Ground cinnamon

Ground cumin

Equipment

You really don't need a lot of special equipment to make these meals. However, here's a list of some items that will speed your preparation and cooking and make your life easier.

Food Processor

A food processor or mini-chopper will help quickly slice and chop and also blend foods together.

Garlic Press

Some of the newer ones allow you to crush garlic without peeling the cloves. I also use it to crush fresh ginger.

Knives

Sharp knives are important for fast and accurate cutting. A blunt knife can be dangerous. It can slip or slide when you are trying to slice. Three different types are all you really need for most cutting tasks: a 4-inch paring knife, an 8-inch chef's knife, and a small serrated knife for fruit or tomatoes.

Meat Thermometer

I love the new style that uses a probe. The cord is connected to a dial that sits on the work surface. The dial is easy to read and doesn't get hot or dirty. With the cord, it works well for items on the stove, in the oven, or under the broiler.

Microwave Ovens

Use this fast-cooking appliance. And remember, any dish that's microwave safe is dishwasher safe, too. Be careful; it's easy to overcook food. Food continues to cook several seconds after it has been removed from the oven.

Pots and Pans

You can make most of the meals in this book using a medium 9–10-inch nonstick skillet, a large 3–4-quart saucepan, and a wok. Nonstick skillets are essential, as these recipes are designed using small amounts of oil. If you follow the instructions, your food will not stick.

Scales

Small kitchen scales are very handy and not expensive.

Vegetable Peeler

For easy peeling, make sure yours is sharp. These are actually little knives and should be replaced as they start to get blunt.

Quick Cooking Tips and Helpful Hints

Each recipe has a Helpful Hints section. Knowing what to substitute, the best way to prepare ingredients, or some other shortcut can make a big difference to the time it takes to get your meal on the table.

Chopping Fresh Herbs

To quickly chop herbs, snip the leaves off the stem with scissors.

Crisp Stir-Fry

For crisp, not steamed, stir-fried vegetables, make sure your wok or skillet is very hot. The oil should be smoking. Let the vegetables sit a minute before tossing to allow the wok to regain its heat.

Dried Spices and Herbs

If using dried spices, make sure the jar is less than 6 months old. To bring out the flavor of the dried herbs, chop them with fresh parsley. The juice from the parsley will help release the flavor of the herbs.

Electric Cooking

To get a quick high/low response from electric rings, heat two rings, one on medium-high and the other on low. Move the pan back and forth between them.

Fluffy Rice

I like to cook my rice like pasta, using a saucepan of boiling water that's large enough for the rice to roll freely. Use this method or follow the directions on the rice package.

Food Processor

To use the food processor for a recipe without having to stop to wash the bowl, first chop the dry ingredients (such as nuts), and then the wet ones (such as onion). You won't have to stop in the middle of preparing the ingredients.

Fresh Ginger

To chop fresh ginger quickly, cut it into small cubes and press through a garlic press with large holes. If using a press with small holes, just capture the juice that is squeezed out; it will give enough flavor for the recipe.

Parmesan Cheese

Buy good-quality Parmesan cheese and grate it yourself or chop it in the food processor. Freeze extra for quick use later. You can quickly spoon out what you need and leave the rest frozen.

Peeling Shrimp

Buying peeled shrimp saves time otherwise spent shelling them yourself.

Slices and Weight

To determine the weight of sliced cheese or packaged meats, look at the package weight or nutritional analysis to determine how much each slice weighs.

Timely Stir-Fry

To keep from looking back at a recipe as you stir-fry the ingredients, line them up on a chopping board or plate in the order of use. You will know which ingredient comes next.

Washing Herbs

The quickest way to wash watercress, arugula, parsley, or basil is to place the bunch, head first, into a bowl of water. Leave for a minute, then lift out and shake dry. The dirt and sand will be left behind.

Washing Mushrooms

To clean whole mushrooms, wipe them with damp paper towel.

Tips for Eating Out

One of the biggest challenges to making sure we eat healthily is that 60 percent of our meals are prepared outside the home. We eat out, bring in, and eat on the run. Use the recipes in this book as a guide to eating out. Once you understand the types of food and proportion sizes, you will be able to order from the menu with confidence. Here are some hints and tips to eat well in spite of your schedule:

- Avoid all deep-fried foods.

- Avoid sugary drinks. Opt for water, unsweetened iced tea, or diet drinks.

- Plain, soft tacos or tortilla-filled wraps are fine as long as they aren't filled with rice and beans. Ask for whole wheat, if possible.

- Roasted or broiled meats are best. Make sure you include vegetables with your meal. Stay away from sugar-based sauces, especially barbecue sauce and most glazes.

- Many meals are loaded with carbs. Order two vegetables instead of a starch. Most restaurants are used to substituting this way.

- Ask for your salad dressing on the side. Most salads come swimming in dressing. You'll be surprised how far 1 tablespoon of dressing will go. Or just dip your vegetables into the dressing on the side.

- If you order dessert, share it with the table or make sure you don't have a starch during dinner. Better still, order a fresh fruit salad or berries.

- Have a good-carb snack (vegetables, a few nuts, a slice of low-carbohydrate cheese) before you go out to eat. This will help you avoid the basket of bread on the table while you're waiting for your meal.

- Ask for the bread basket to be brought to the table with the main course to save munching on the bread while you are ordering.

- Don't go out for drinks on an empty stomach. One drink will make you hungry, and you'll eat the first thing you can find. Have a healthy snack before you go out. (See page 25 for a snack list.) If you think it will be a long night, start with sparkling water with a piece of lemon or lime or a diet soft drink first.

- Fast food can be fine. Order broiled chicken or fish and discard the bread. Or eat it as an open sandwich using half a roll. Order a salad with the dressing on the side. Stay away from fries, baked potatoes, and potato chips.

- Chinese food can be loaded with sugar. Order stir-fried meats and vegetables or skewered meats, and avoid soups with wontons. Avoid egg rolls, ribs in thick sauce, and noodles. It is refreshing to see that some restaurants are offering brown rice as an alternative to white rice.

- Italian food doesn't have to mean a plate of pasta. Order an antipasto platter or any of the meats, salads, or vegetables.

- French food can be very healthy. Order clear soups, salads, vegetables, meats, or seafood, but avoid heavy sauces and bread.

- Japanese sushi is based on rice—very often with sugar added to it. Try miso soup or any of the cooked meats and vegetables instead.

- Mexican food can be high in saturated fat and carbohydrates. Fajitas (1 tortilla) with the garnishes, broiled meats, and salads are fine. Avoid rice, refried beans, and nachos.

SIZING IT UP

Watch portion size when eating out. Many restaurant servings are large enough for two meals. Here's a guide to help you size up what you should be eating.

3 ounces cooked meat, poultry, or fish	a deck of cards
1 1/2 ounces cheese	6 dice
1 tortilla	a small (7-inch) plate
1 muffin	a large egg
1 teaspoon butter	a thumb tip
2 tablespoons peanut butter	a golf ball

Information from *Food Insight News* published by IFIC (International Food Information Council)

Quick Snacks

Snacks are important little meals that will help you through the day, especially during the first Quick Start phase. They can prevent that sinking feeling at 4 or 5 p.m. when your energy is low, or the mid-morning, is-it-time-for-lunch clock watching.

Knowing what to snack on and how to have it handy can help prevent raids on the vending machine to satiate sweet cravings.

Here are some ideas:

The remains of an extra large lunch salad, which you can take back to your office or home

- 1 ounce low-fat cheese (mozzarella, small round individually packed, wax-covered low-fat cheese)

- 1 ounce low-fat cottage cheese

- 1 ounce nuts, such as almonds, pecans and, walnuts ($1/4$ cup). Keep small packages of nuts, the type that are found in the baking section of the supermarket, in your drawer at work, pocketbook or briefcase. They're easy to carry around and contain portion-size amounts.

- 2 ounces deli meats, such as lean ham, turkey, chicken, or roast beef

- 1 hard-boiled egg. Keep a few hard-boiled eggs on hand for snacks. They will need to be refrigerated at the office.

- 1 ounce sunflower seeds

- 6 olives

- Any vegetables such as cucumber slices, celery sticks, broccoli, or cauliflower florets and sliced bell pepper

quick start

THIS TWO-WEEK MEAL PLAN IS DESIGNED TO START YOU OFF ON CUTTING CARBS FROM YOUR MEALS.

When I give cooking classes and show these meals, the response always surprises me. "You mean I can eat all of that?" is the usual response. Knowing the quantities of each type of food you can eat will help you to build your own recipes to fit your lifestyle.

I have organized the menus into a meal-at-a-glance chart with some easy and quick meals mid-week and those that take a little more time for the weekends. They are arranged to give variety throughout the day and over the days of the week.

Breakfast

There's plenty of variety in these breakfasts to fit all tastes, from Microwave Marinara Scramble to Turkey Salsa Roll. Pick the ones you like and use them for this two-week period.

Mid-Morning Snack

When you first start reducing carbs, you will need to eat a mid-morning snack. I've included a section with some suggestions. (See page 25.)

Lunch

There's a lunch for any occasion here—quick-take lunches that can be eaten at home or taken with you, more elaborate lunches for when you have more time or friends come round.

Enjoy Spanish Tuna-Stuffed Tomatoes and Nutty Chicken Minestrone. These meals can be made at home and taken to work. They are commonly found on most lunch menus. If you are eating out, use these recipes as a guide for the portions you should eat.

I usually order my salads with the dressing on the side. Most salads come swimming in dressing. I find that 1 tablespoon of dressing gently coats the salad without overpowering it. So, I prefer to add the dressing to the salad myself. (See pages 23–24 for more tips on eating out.)

Mid-Afternoon Snack

When you first start reducing carbs, you will need to eat a mid-afternoon snack. (See page 25.)

Dinner

Do you feel like Italian, French, or American food tonight? There's something from each ethnic group – Tuscan Chicken, Roasted Salmon, and Herb Sauce, and Chicken Burgers with Warm Mushroom Salad are some of the tempting meals.

For those days when you are really pressed for time, select Savory Sage Chicken or Jamaican Jerk Pork from the Super Speed Suppers section of the book.

For weekends when you have more time and want something special try, the Dijon Chicken with Crunchy Couscous or Garlic-Stuffed Steak from the Weekends section of the book.

How low is low carb? It's important to reduce carbohydrate intake low enough for a period of time so that you eliminate the peaks of insulin secretion. Following the Quick Start 14-Day Meal Plan, you will consume an average of 35–45 grams of carbohydrates per day. Carbohydrate percentage is based on carbohydrates less fiber consumed, which is the normal way of calculating carbohydrate consumption. The balance of these meals is 11 percent of calories from carbs, 40 percent of calories from low-fat proteins, and 36 percent of calories from mono-unsaturated fat and 11 percent of calories from saturated fat.

To achieve the correct balance, I have structured the recipes as complete meals. Whatever meal you pick, it's best to stay with the entire menu given.

quick start 14-day plan at a glance

week 1	breakfast	lunch	dinner
sunday	Bacon and Cheese Crêpes 31	Sicilian Baked Mushrooms and Sausage 39	Dijon Chicken with Crunchy Couscous 143
monday	Microwave Eggs Parmesan...................32	Chicken with Dill Mustard...................40	Greek Shrimp with Feta Cheese 127
tuesday	Mushroom, Turkey, and Tarragon Omelette.......33	Cheese and Chicken Bundles.....................41	Hot Pepper Shrimp.......47
wednesday	Turkey Salsa Roll...........34	Nutty Chicken Minestrone 42	Mediterranean Baked Fish...........................48
thursday	Microwave Marinara Scramble.....................35	Spanish Tuna-Stuffed Tomatoes....................43	Savory Sage Chicken...................129
friday	Smoked Salmon -Stuffed Celery..........................36	Crunchy Oriental Chicken Salad...........................44	Jamaican Jerk Pork........128
saturday	Sausage and Artichoke Frittata........................37	Crab Gratin...................45	Chicken Burgers with Warm Mushroom Salad.........50

week 2	breakfast	lunch	dinner
sunday	Bacon and Cheese Crêpes 31	Sicilian Baked Mushrooms and Sausage.................39	Garlic Stuffed-Steak 144
monday	Microwave Eggs Parmesan.....................32	Chicken with Dill Mustard.......................40	Crab Cakes and Slaw.....................51
tuesday	Mushroom, Turkey, and Tarragon Omelette........33	Cheese and Chicken Bundles.......................41	Pork Escalopes with Spinach and Mushrooms.................52
wednesday	Turkey Salsa Roll...........34	Nutty Chicken Minestrone..................42	Roasted Salmon and Herb Sauce...........................53
thursday	Microwave Marinara Scramble.....................35	Spanish Tuna-Stuffed Tomatoes......................43	Tuscan Chicken............54
friday	Smoked Salmon-Stuffed Celery...........................36	Crunchy Oriental Chicken Salad............................44	Savory Sage Chicken......................129
saturday	Sausage and Artichoke Frittata........................37	Crab Gratin....................45	Veal Saltimbocca...........146

quick start
breakfasts

bacon and cheese crêpes

Making eggs into thin crêpes is the secret to this dish. Be sure to use a good nonstick frying pan for best results.

bacon and cheese crêpes

1 cup egg substitute

Freshly ground black pepper

Olive oil spray

6 ounces lean ham, cut into
    1-inch strips

3 ounces grated part-skim milk
    mozzarella cheese

1 medium tomato, sliced

Pre-heat broiler. Mix egg substitute with pepper to taste. Heat a medium nonstick frying pan on medium-high heat. Spray with olive oil spray and pour half the egg substitute into frying pan and spread to make a thin layer. Leave to cook for 2 minutes. Turn over for 1 minute.

Remove from heat to a foil-lined baking tray. Repeat with second half of egg mixture. Sprinkle bacon and cheese over crêpes. Fold over once and place under broiler about 10 inches from heat. Broil for 2 minutes or until cheese melts. Carefully slide on to a plate, place sliced tomatoes on the side, and serve.

Makes 2 servings.

Per serving: 335 calories, 43.2 grams protein, 7.0 grams carbohydrate, 14.2 grams fat (7.5 saturated), 73 milligrams cholesterol, 1227 milligrams sodium, 0 grams fiber

helpful hint

- Make these crêpes ahead, and fill and warm in a microwave oven when needed.

countdown

- Pre-heat broiler.
- Make egg base.
- Complete recipe.

shopping list

FRUIT AND VEG

  1 medium tomato

DAIRY

  1 package grated part-skim
    milk mozzarella cheese

DELI

  6 ounces lean ham

STAPLES

  Egg substitute

  Olive oil spray

  Black peppercorns

microwave eggs parmesan

Here is another quick microwave breakfast. The timing of this dish depends on the power of your microwave oven. Also, some like their eggs dry, others wet. Select the timing according to your preference. Remember the eggs will continue to cook for about 1 minute after they are removed from the oven.

helpful hints

● *Buy good-quality Parmesan cheese and grate it yourself or chop it in the food processor. Freeze extra for quick use. You can quickly spoon out what you need and leave the rest frozen.*

countdown

● *Make eggs.*
● *Arrange salad on 2 plates.*

shopping list

FRUIT AND VEG
 1 medium tomato
 1 small head romaine lettuce
DELI
 4 ounces smoked turkey
STAPLES
 Eggs (6 needed)
 Parmesan cheese
 Salt
 Black peppercorns

microwave eggs parmesan

4 egg whites
2 large eggs
¼ pound smoked turkey, cut into
  small cubes
2 tablespoons grated Parmesan
  cheese
Salt and freshly ground black
  pepper
Several romaine lettuce leaves
1 medium tomato, sliced

Place 2 egg whites and 1 whole egg in a microwave-safe bowl about 7 inches in diameter. Add 2 tablespoons turkey, 1 tablespoon Parmesan cheese, and salt and pepper to taste. Whisk with a fork. Microwave on high for 1 minute. Stir and microwave for 30 seconds and stir. For drier eggs, microwave 30 seconds more.

Arrange lettuce leaves on 2 plates and place tomato slices on top. Spoon eggs on to plate. Using the same bowl, repeat for second serving. *Makes 2 servings.*

Per serving: 255 calories, 35.3 grams protein, 4.5 grams carbohydrate, 10.9 grams fat (4.0 saturated), 260 milligrams cholesterol, 394 milligrams sodium, 0.2 grams fiber

mushroom, turkey, and tarragon omelette

Omelettes take only minutes to make. A perfect omelette is golden on the top with a delicate creamy center. The secret is to cook it over medium-high heat for only a couple of minutes.

mushroom, turkey, and tarragon omelette

4 egg whites

2 large whole eggs

4 ounces smoked turkey breast, cut into 1-inch cubes

1 teaspoon dried tarragon

Salt and freshly ground black pepper

Olive oil spray

4 ounces thinly sliced portobello mushrooms

1 medium tomato, cut into 1-inch pieces

Place eggs and egg whites in a bowl and stir in turkey, tarragon, and salt and pepper to taste. Heat a medium nonstick skillet over medium-high heat and spray with olive oil. Sauté mushrooms and tomatoes for 2 minutes and remove. Pour in the egg mixture. Let the eggs set for about 30 seconds. Tip the pan and lightly move the eggs so that they set completely. Cook for 1½ minutes or until eggs are set. Cook a few seconds longer for firmer eggs.

Place the mushrooms and tomatoes on half the omelette and fold the omelette in half. Slide out of the pan by tipping the pan and holding a plate vertically against the side of the pan. Turn pan and plate to invert the omelette on to the plate. Cut in half and serve on 2 plates.

Makes 2 servings.

> Per serving: 228 calories, 31.5 grams protein, 4.7 grams carbohydrate, 9.3 grams fat (2.5 saturated), 253 milligrams cholesterol, 215 milligrams sodium, 0 grams fiber

helpful hints

- *Any herb can be used.*
- *Dried tarragon is called for in the recipe. If using dried herbs, make sure the jar is less than 6 months old.*
- *For best results, use a good-quality nonstick pan.*

countdown

- *Prepare ingredients.*
- *Complete omelette.*

shopping list

FRUIT AND VEG

4 ounces portobello mushrooms

1 medium tomato

DELI

4 ounces smoked turkey breast

STAPLES:

Eggs (6 needed)

Olive oil spray

Dried tarragon

Salt

Black peppercorns

turkey salsa roll

Sliced turkey roll stuffed with Cheddar cheese and topped with salsa is a breakfast that can be made ahead and warmed in 1 minute in a microwave oven before eating.

turkey salsa roll

8 ounces sliced, smoked turkey breast

2 ounces grated reduced-fat Cheddar cheese

1 cup no-sugar-added tomato salsa

Place turkey slices on the work surface or a plate and sprinkle each slice with cheese. Roll up slices and divide between 2 plates. Microwave each plate on high for 1 minute or until cheese melts. If not using a microwave oven, place turkey rolls on a foil-lined baking sheet under a broiler for 1 minute. Remove plates from microwave and spoon salsa over the top.
Makes 2 servings.

Per serving: 310 calories, 44.0 grams protein, 10.4 grams carbohydrate, 8.5 grams fat (4.2 saturated), 90 milligrams cholesterol, 1036 milligrams sodium, 4.0 grams fiber

helpful hints

- To help the morning rush, stuff the turkey the night before and warm just before eating.

countdown

- Prepare ingredients.
- Complete dish.

shopping list

DAIRY
1 small package grated reduced-fat Cheddar cheese

STAPLES:
1 small jar no-sugar-added tomato salsa

microwave marinara scramble

This breakfast takes just minutes to make in a microwave oven. A rich, thick marinara sauce gives these scrambled eggs a taste of Naples.

The timing of this dish depends on the power of your microwave oven. Also, some like their eggs dry, others wet. Select the timing according to your preference. Remember the eggs will continue to cook for about 1 minute after they are removed from the oven.

microwave marinara scramble

5 ounces washed, ready-to-eat
   baby spinach
1/4 pound lean ham, cut into 1-inch
   pieces
1 cup egg substitute
1/4 cup low-salt, no-sugar-added
   marinara sauce
Salt and freshly ground black
   pepper
6 tablespoons grated part-skim
   milk mozzarella cheese

Place spinach and ham in a microwave-safe bowl and microwave on high for 2 minutes. Divide between 2 plates.

Combine egg substitute and marinara sauce together in a microwave-safe bowl. Season with salt and pepper to taste. Cover with plastic wrap or a plate. Microwave on high for 4 minutes. Stir and divide in half. Place each portion on top of the spinach and ham. Sprinkle 2 tablespoons mozzarella cheese on top of each portion.

Makes 2 servings.

Per serving: 250 calories, 33.6 grams protein,
10.6 grams carbohydrate, 8.6 grams fat
(4.0 saturated), 43 milligrams cholesterol,
1127 milligrams sodium, 3.6 grams fiber

helpful hints

● If you don't have a microwave oven, sauté the spinach for 1 minute in a small skillet and remove to a plate. Scramble the eggs in the same pan.

● If baby spinach is unavailable, use any type of spinach or lettuce.

countdown

● Microwave spinach.
● Microwave scrambled eggs.

shopping list

FRUIT AND VEG
   1 bag washed, ready-to-eat baby spinach (5 ounces needed)
DAIRY
   1 small package grated part-skim milk mozzarella cheese
DELI
   1/4 pound lean ham
GROCERY
   1 small jar low-salt, no-sugar-added marinara sauce

staples

   Egg substitute (8 ounces needed)
   Salt
   Black peppercorns

smoked salmon-stuffed celery

If you're in a hurry, make this breakfast the night before and take it with you to eat on the run.

smoked salmon-stuffed celery

$^3/_4$ *pound smoked salmon*
$^1/_4$ *pound soured cream*
2 tablespoons snipped chives
Freshly ground black pepper
8 medium celery stalks

Chop salmon. This can be done in a food processor or by hand. Mix with the soured cream and chives. Add black pepper to taste. Spread into celery and cut stalks into 2-inch pieces. Divide between 2 plates.
Makes 2 servings.

Per serving: 290 calories, 33.4 grams protein, 13.2 grams carbohydrate, 13.9 grams fat (4.9 saturated), 53 milligrams cholesterol, 1625 milligrams sodium, 4.0 grams fiber

sausage and artichoke frittata

Plump, juicy frittatas take about 15 minutes to make. They can be made ahead and eaten at room temperature or reheated in a microwave oven. They differ from omelettes. An omelette is cooked fast over high heat making it creamy and runny, while a frittata is cooked slowly over low heat, making it firm and set. A frittata needs to be cooked on both sides. Some people flip it in the pan. A much easier way is to place it in a pre-heated oven to finish cooking or under the broiler for half a minute.

Low-fat turkey sausages are available in the supermarkets. If you have a local butcher who makes his own sausages you may be able to pick different flavorings, ranging from mild to spicy hot. Choose whichever type suits your palate.

sausage and artichoke frittata

2 teaspoons olive oil
*2 low-fat turkey sausages, cut into
   ¹/₂-inch slices (6 ounces)*
4 egg whites
2 large whole eggs
*³/₄ cup drained marinated
   artichoke hearts, cut in half*
1 tablespoon freeze-dried chives
*Salt and freshly ground black
   pepper*

Pre-heat oven to 400 degrees. Heat olive oil in an 7–8-inch nonstick skillet on medium-high heat. Sauté sausage for 3 minutes. Mix egg whites, whole eggs, and artichokes together. Add chives and salt and pepper to taste. Reduce heat to medium and pour egg mixture into pan. Spread to cover sausage and artichokes. Leave to set on the bottom for 3 minutes. Place in oven for 7 minutes or until eggs set. If you like drier eggs, leave for 1 further minute.
Makes 2 servings.

Per serving: 337 calories, 29.0 grams protein,
7.0 grams carbohydrate, 21.3 grams fat
(4.2 saturated), 258 milligrams cholesterol,
893 milligrams sodium, 1.0 grams fiber

helpful hints

- *Egg substitute can be used instead of 2 whole eggs and 6 egg whites.*

countdown

- *Pre-heat oven to 400 degrees.*
- *Prepare ingredients.*
- *Make frittata.*

shopping list

MEAT
   *1 small package low-fat
      turkey sausages (6 ounces
      needed)*
GROCERY
   *1 small jar marinated
      artichoke hearts*
   *1 small container freeze-
      dried chives*
STAPLES:
   Eggs (6 needed)
   Olive oil
   Salt
   Black peppercorns

quick start
lunches

sicilian baked mushrooms and sausage

Mushrooms baked with garlic and sausage and topped with cheese and breadcrumbs is a dish that originates from Palermo in Sicily. The dish can be baked in an oven or takes only minutes in a microwave.

sicilian baked mushrooms and sausage

Olive oil spray

³/₄ pound low-fat turkey sausages, cut into 1-inch pieces

3³/₄ cups thinly sliced button mushrooms

4 garlic cloves, crushed

¹/₈ teaspoon crushed chiles

Salt and freshly ground black pepper

¹/₄ cup chopped fresh parsley

2 tablespoons breadcrumbs

3 tablespoons grated Parmesan cheese

Spray a 10-inch microwave-safe pie plate with olive oil spray. Add the sausages and microwave on high for 2 minutes. Remove from microwave and pour off fat. Add mushrooms, garlic, and chile. Add salt and pepper to taste. Sprinkle parsley over mushrooms. Sprinkle breadcrumbs and Parmesan cheese on top. Microwave on high for 5 minutes. Or place in a pre-heated 400-degree oven for 15 minutes. Divide between 2 plates.

Makes 2 servings.

Per serving: 388 calories, 33.7 grams protein, 11.2 grams carbohydrate, 21.5 grams fat (7.0 saturated), 94 milligrams cholesterol, 1273 milligrams sodium, 0 grams fiber

helpful hints

- Any combination of mushrooms can be used.
- Buy sliced mushrooms or slice in a food processor.
- Crushed chiles can be found in the spice section of the supermarket.
- Buy good-quality Parmesan cheese and grate it yourself or chop it in the food processor. Freeze extra for quick use. You can spoon out what you need and leave the rest frozen.

countdown

- If using an oven, pre-heat to 400 degrees.
- Prepare ingredients.
- Make mushrooms.

shopping list

FRUIT AND VEG

10 ounces button mushrooms, sliced

1 small bunch fresh parsley

MEAT

³/₄ pound low-fat turkey sausages

GROCERY

1 small jar crushed chiles

1 small container plain breadcrumbs

STAPLES:

Olive oil spray

Parmesan cheese

Garlic

Salt

Black peppercorns

chicken with dill mustard

This lunch of sliced chicken breast topped with a dill mustard sauce and crunchy sliced celery requires no cooking and can be assembled the night before. It's also a good recipe for leftover chicken.

chicken with dill mustard

helpful hints

- Dried dill is called for in the recipe. If using dried herbs, make sure the jar is less than 6 months old.

countdown

- Prepare ingredients.
- Complete dish.

shopping list

DELI
  $^3/_4$ pound thick-sliced (about $^1/_4$-inch thick) deli chicken breast
STAPLES
  Celery (12 stalks needed)
  Dijon mustard
  Dried dill
  Mayonnaise

$^3/_4$ pound thick-sliced (about $^1/_4$ inch) deli chicken breast
3 tablespoons Dijon mustard
1$^1/_2$ tablespoons mayonnaise
1$^1/_2$ teaspoons dried dill
12 medium celery stalks, thinly sliced

Divide chicken between 2 plates. Mix mustard, mayonnaise, and dill together and spread half the mixture over the chicken. Place celery slices on top and cover with remaining sauce.
Makes 2 servings.

Per serving: 440 calories, 57.9 grams protein, 19.4 grams carbohydrate, 18.5 grams fat (2.9 saturated), 148 milligrams cholesterol, 1146 milligrams sodium, 6.0 grams fiber

cheese and chicken bundles

Roasted chicken, blue cheese, walnuts, and yogurt blend together to make a tasty spread that is rolled into lettuce leaves. These little bundles can be made ahead and taken to eat on the run.

cheese and chicken bundles

2 ounces blue cheese, crumbled
¼ cup nonfat plain yogurt
2 tablespoons walnut pieces
½ pound roasted chicken strips
Several romaine lettuce leaves
   (about 6)
4 medium celery stalks

Place blue cheese, yogurt, walnuts, and chicken in the bowl of a food processor fitted with a chopping blade. Process to a spreadable consistency. Place lettuce leaves on work surface or a board and spread chicken mixture on leaves. Roll up lengthways and wrap in foil or greaseproof paper. Cut celery stalks into 2-inch pieces and serve on the side.
Makes 2 servings.

Per serving: 411 calories, 46.9 grams protein, 13.3 grams carbohydrate, 21.3 grams fat (7.2 saturated), 118 milligrams cholesterol, 652 milligrams sodium, 3.2 grams fiber

helpful hints

- *Any large lettuce leaves can be used.*
- *Buy plain roasted chicken strips. Stay away from honey roasted or barbecue chicken.*

countdown

- *Prepare ingredients.*
- *Make bundles.*

shopping list

FRUIT AND VEG
   1 small head romaine lettuce
DAIRY
   1 small carton nonfat plain
     yogurt
   1 small package blue cheese
MEAT
   1 package roasted chicken
     strips (pound needed)
GROCERY
   1 small package walnut pieces
STAPLES
   Celery

nutty chicken minestrone

This minestrone is a refreshing blend of flavors using fresh vegetables, chicken and pistachio nuts combined with the perfume of fresh basil. Minestra is Italian for soup. Minestrone is a thick soup that can be made in 20 minutes using bought cooked chicken breasts. Leftover chicken can be used for this recipe. Look for shelled pistachio nuts. They are now available in most supermarkets.

nutty chicken minestrone

2 teaspoons olive oil

1/4 cup grated carrots

1/4 cup celery stalk, sliced

1 medium tomato, diced (1 cup)

1 1/2 cups fat-free, low-sodium
    chicken broth

1 1/2 cups water

1/2 pound roasted, ready-to-eat
    chicken strips

Salt and freshly ground black
    pepper

1/4 pound washed, ready-to-eat
    spinach

1/4 cup fresh basil

2 tablespoons freshly grated
    Parmesan cheese

2 tablespoons coarsely chopped
    pistachio nuts

Heat the oil in a large saucepan on medium-high heat. Add the carrot and celery. Sauté for 5 minutes. Do not brown the vegetables. Stir the vegetables gently, being careful not to break them up. Add the tomato, chicken stock, and water. The liquid should cover the vegetables. Add more water, if needed.

Bring to a simmer and partially cover with a lid, leaving space for steam to escape. Simmer for 10 minutes. Add the chicken and simmer for 5 more minutes. Add salt and pepper to taste. Remove from heat. Stir in the spinach and basil. Leave to stand for 1 minute. Spoon into 2 soup bowls. Sprinkle each bowl with Parmesan cheese and pistachio nuts. *Makes 2 servings.*

Per serving: 379 calories, 46.6 grams protein, 10.1 grams carbohydrate, 18.4 grams fat (4.3 saturated), 103 milligrams cholesterol, 731 milligrams sodium, 1.3 grams fiber

helpful hints

- Walnuts, pecans, or almonds can be substituted for pistachio nuts.
- Buy good-quality Parmesan cheese and grate it yourself or chop it in the food processor. Freeze extra for quick use. You can spoon out what you need and leave the rest frozen.
- Grated carrots are available in the fruit and veg section of the supermarket.

countdown

- Prepare ingredients.
- Make soup.

shopping list

FRUIT AND VEG

1 small pack grated carrots

1 bag washed, ready-to-eat
    spinach

1 medium tomato

1 small bunch basil

MEAT

1/2 pound roasted chicken
    strips or pieces

GROCERY

1 small package shelled
    pistachio nuts

STAPLES

Olive oil

Parmesan cheese

Fat-free, low-sodium chicken
    broth (12 ounces needed)

Celery

Salt

Black peppercorns

spanish tuna-stuffed tomatoes

Olives, pimientos, and almonds mix with tuna to make a Spanish tuna salad. This is also a good recipe for leftover chicken or other seafood.

spanish tuna-stuffed tomatoes

2 large tomatoes

2 tablespoons mayonnaise

Freshly ground black pepper

9 ounces canned tuna packed in
water, drained

6 stoned green olives, sliced

1 cup sliced sweet pimiento,
drained

2¹/₂ tablespoons flaked almonds
(1 ounce)

Several lettuce leaves, washed and
torn into bite-sized pieces

Cut tomatoes in half, scoop out pulp and seeds, and take a thin slice off the rounded bottom of each half. This will help the tomatoes sit straight on the plate. Set the tomato halves aside. Mix mayonnaise with black pepper to taste. Add the tuna, olives, pimiento, and almonds. Mix to combine. Taste for seasoning and add more, if necessary.

Place the lettuce on 2 plates and the tomato halves on the lettuce. Fill the tomatoes with the tuna salad. Serve extra salad on the lettuce. *Makes 2 servings.*

Per serving: 404 calories, 39.2 grams protein,
12.6 grams carbohydrate, 22.5 grams fat
(2.3 saturated), 61 milligrams cholesterol,
945 milligrams sodium, 0.2 grams fiber

helpful hints

● *Use good-quality, water-packed, canned tuna.*

● *To help the tomato halves sit straight, cut a thin slice from the rounded ends.*

● *Any type of lettuce can be used.*

countdown

● *Prepare ingredients.*

● *Make recipe.*

shopping list

FRUIT AND VEG

2 large tomatoes

1 small head lettuce

GROCERY

9 ounces canned tuna
packed in water

1 jar stoned green olives
(6 needed)

1 small jar sweet pimientos

1 small package flaked
almonds (1 ounce needed)

STAPLES

Mayonnaise

Black peppercorns

crunchy oriental chicken salad

Roasted or rotisserie chicken takes on a new dimension in this quick salad. Adding ginger and soy sauce to a bottled oil and vinegar dressing gives it an Oriental flavor.

crunchy oriental chicken salad

helpful hints

- *Any type of lettuce can be used.*

countdown

- *Prepare ingredients.*
- *Assemble salad.*

shopping list

FRUIT AND VEG

1 bag washed, ready-to-eat gourmet salad leaves

1 small bunch scallions

MEAT

1/2 pound roasted, ready-to-eat chicken pieces

GROCERY

1 small can sliced water chestnuts

1 jar ground ginger

STAPLES

Olive oil and vinegar dressing

Low-sodium soy sauce

1/2 pound roasted, ready-to-eat chicken pieces

1 cup drained, sliced water chestnuts

4 scallions, sliced

3 tablespoons olive oil and vinegar dressing

2 teaspoons low-sodium soy sauce

1/2 teaspoon ground ginger

4 cups washed, ready-to-eat mixed gourmet salad leaves

Place chicken pieces, water chestnuts, and scallions in a large bowl. Mix dressing, soy sauce, and ginger together, and pour over chicken. Toss well. Divide salad leaves between 2 plates and spoon chicken salad on top. *Makes 2 servings.*

Per serving: 378 calories, 38.7 grams protein, 17.3 grams carbohydrate, 18.1 grams fat (3.1 saturated), 96 milligrams cholesterol, 437 milligrams sodium, 4.6 grams fiber

crab gratin

Good-quality crabmeat is the secret to this quick lunch. Fresh crabmeat from the seafood counter would be best; but if this is difficult to find, use pasteurized crabmeat.

crab gratin

3 tablespoons mayonnaise

2 tablespoons lemon juice or water

$^3/_4$ pound crabmeat (about 2$^1/_2$ cups)

Salt and freshly ground black pepper

2 large tomatoes, cut into $^1/_2$-inch slices

$^1/_4$ cup grated reduced-fat Cheddar cheese

Pre-heat broiler. Mix mayonnaise and lemon juice together in a small bowl. Add crabmeat and flake with a fork as it's mixed with the mayonnaise. Add salt and pepper to taste. Place tomato slices on foil-lined baking tray. Spoon crab over tomatoes and sprinkle cheese on top. Place under broiler for 2–3 minutes or until cheese melts. Remove to 2 plates and serve. *Makes 2 servings.*

Per serving: 382 calories, 37.1 grams protein, 9.1 grams carbohydrate, 21.2 grams fat (4.5 saturated), 149 milligrams cholesterol, 746 milligrams sodium, 0 grams fiber

helpful hints

● *Frozen crab can be used. The flavor will be fine; the crabmeat will be soft.*

● *Pasteurized crabmeat can be found in the refrigerated section of the seafood department.*

countdown

● *Pre-heat broiler.*
● *Prepare ingredients.*
● *Make gratin.*

shopping list

FRUIT AND VEG

   2 large tomatoes

DAIRY

   1 small package grated reduced-fat Cheddar cheese

SEAFOOD

   $^3/_4$ pound crabmeat

STAPLES

   Lemon

   Mayonnaise

   Salt

   Black peppercorns

quick start
dinners

hot pepper shrimp

Hot, spicy shrimp with lots of garlic are a popular Spanish tapas dish. The shrimp dish is normally served on its own for tapas; but by adding a quick salad, it becomes an entire meal. Endive is a small cigar-shaped head of lettuce that is creamy white. It has tightly packed leaves and can be cleaned by wiping the outer leaves with damp paper towel. The leaves will turn brown if soaked in water.

hot pepper shrimp

10 ounces washed, ready-to-eat spinach (about 8 cups)
6 garlic cloves, crushed
Salt and freshly ground black pepper
1 tablespoon olive oil
Pinch crushed chili flakes
3/4 pound shrimp, peeled
2 tablespoons chopped fresh parsley

Place spinach and 3 crushed garlic cloves in a large microwave-safe bowl. Microwave on high for 3 minutes. Add salt and pepper to taste. Toss well. Divide between 2 plates. Heat a medium nonstick skillet on medium-high heat. Add olive oil and chili flakes.

When oil is hot, add shrimp and remaining 3 crushed garlic cloves. Toss shrimp in oil for 2–3 minutes or until shrimp are no longer translucent. Remove from heat and sprinkle with parsley and salt and pepper to taste. Spoon over spinach including pan juices. *Makes 2 servings.*

Per serving: 299 calories, 41.4 grams protein, 11.5 grams carbohydrate, 10.7 grams fat (1.5 saturated), 260 milligrams cholesterol, 426 milligrams sodium, 7.2 grams fiber

red bell pepper and endive salad

2 medium heads Belgian endive lettuce, sliced
1 medium red bell pepper, sliced into 1-inch strips
2 tablespoons olive oil and vinegar dressing
Salt and freshly ground black pepper

Wipe endive with damp paper towel. Cut off about 1/2 inch from the bottom or flat end and discard. Cut endive into 1/2-inch slices and place in a small bowl. Add red bell pepper strips to bowl. Drizzle with dressing and add salt and pepper to taste. Toss well.
Makes 2 servings.

Per serving: 253 calories, 1.3 grams protein, 7.1 grams carbohydrate, 25.2 grams fat (4.4 saturated), 0 milligrams cholesterol, 239 milligrams sodium, 0 grams fiber

helpful hints

- Shelled shrimp are available at most supermarket seafood counters. The slightly higher cost is worth the time saved.
- A quick way to chop parsley is to wash, dry, and snip the leaves with scissors right off the stem.
- Any type of lettuce can be used for the salad.

countdown

- Make salad.
- Prepare shrimp.

shopping list

FRUIT AND VEG
1 (10-ounce) bag washed, ready-to-eat spinach
1 medium red bell pepper
1 small bunch parsley
2 medium heads endive lettuce
SEAFOOD
3/4 pound shelled shrimp
GROCERY
1 small jar crushed chili flakes
STAPLES
Olive oil
Garlic
Olive oil and vinegar dressing
Salt
Black peppercorns

mediterranean baked fish

Try a taste of the Mediterranean with this baked grouper topped with pinenuts, olives, and pimiento. An Italian friend does great zucchinis with a hint of melted cheese on top. She told me her secret: grate the zucchinis, using a grater with large holes. They cook faster and taste better. I created this quick zucchini gratin with memories of her wonderful dish.

helpful hints

- Any type of mild white fish fillet can be used in this recipe. Bake about 10 minutes per 1 inch of thickness.
- Grate the zucchinis in a food processor using a julienne cutting blade or use a grater with 1/4-inch holes.

countdown

- Pre-heat oven to 400 degrees.
- Make fish.
- While fish bakes, make zucchinis.
- Assemble salad.

mediterranean baked fish

3/4 pound grouper fillets
Salt and freshly ground black
  pepper
2 teaspoons olive oil
2 tablespoons pinenuts
6 pitted green olives, cut in half
1/2 cup sliced sweet pimiento,
  drained

Pre-heat oven to 400 degrees. Line a baking tray with foil. Rinse fish and pat dry with kitchen paper. Sprinkle fish with salt and pepper to taste. Place on prepared baking tray and drizzle oil on top. Bake for 10 minutes. Spoon pinenuts, olives, and peppers over fish. Return to oven for 10 minutes.
Makes 2 servings.

Per serving: 255 calories, 33.2 grams protein, 2.2 grams carbohydrate, 8.0 grams fat (1.2 saturated), 62 milligrams cholesterol, 373 milligrams sodium, 0 grams fiber

green salad

4 cups washed, ready-to-eat
  lettuce
2 tablespoons olive oil and vinegar
  dressing

Place lettuce in a large bowl and toss with dressing.
Makes 2 servings.

Per serving: 84 calories, 0.6 grams protein, 1.9 grams carbohydrate, 8.5 grams fat (1.3 saturated), 0 milligrams cholesterol, 81 milligrams sodium, 0.3 grams fiber

Chicken Burgers with Mushroom Salad   **p50**

zucchini gratin

1 pound zucchinis, grated
2 tablespoons grated Parmesan
   cheese
Salt and freshly ground black
   pepper
2 teaspoons olive oil

Place zucchinis in a microwave-safe bowl. Microwave on high for 2 minutes. If you do not have a microwave oven, bring a small saucepan of water to the boil and add the zucchinis. Drain as soon as the water comes back to the boil.

Spoon half the zucchinis into a shallow ovenproof dish. Sprinkle 1 tablespoon Parmesan cheese and salt and pepper to taste on top. Cover with remaining zucchinis and finish with Parmesan cheese and salt and pepper to taste. Drizzle olive oil on top. Place in oven with fish for 5 minutes or until cheese melts.
Makes 2 servings.

Per serving: 129 calories, 7.9 grams protein, 8.0 grams carbohydrate, 8.4 grams fat (2.8 saturated), 9 milligrams cholesterol, 219 milligrams sodium, 1.2 grams fiber

shopping list

FRUIT AND VEG
   1 pound zucchinis
   1 bag washed, ready-to-eat
      lettuce
SEAFOOD
   ³/₄ pound grouper fillets
GROCERY
   1 small package pinenuts
      (¹/₂ ounce needed)
   1 small jar pitted green olives
   1 small jar sweet pimientos
STAPLES
   Olive oil
   Olive oil and vinegar dressing
   Parmesan cheese
   Salt
   Black peppercorns

helpful hints

- *Parsley or cilantro can be used instead of basil in the burgers.*
- *Only 2 tablespoons pesto are needed for the burgers. Extra pesto sauce can be frozen.*
- *To save washing up, cook the mushrooms , then remove and use the same pan for the burgers.*
- *A quick way to chop basil is to wash, dry, then snip the leaves with scissors off the stem.*

countdown

- *Sauté mushrooms and remove from skillet.*
- *Prepare chicken burgers while mushrooms cook.*
- *Prepare tomato topping for chicken.*
- *Cook chicken burgers.*

shopping list

FRUIT AND VEG

1 medium tomato
1 small bunch fresh basil
1 small bunch scallions
1/2 pound portobello mushrooms
1 small head radicchio

MEAT

3/4 pound chicken mince

GROCERY

1 small jar prepared pesto sauce

STAPLES

Olive oil spray
Garlic
Olive oil and vinegar dressing
Salt
Black peppercorns

chicken burgers with warm mushroom salad

These burgers are tasty and juicy and take only a few minutes to make. Prepared pesto sauce gives the burgers a taste of Italy and keeps the meat juicy.

chicken burgers

3/4 pound chicken mince
2 tablespoons prepared pesto sauce
1/2 teaspoon freshly ground black pepper
Dash of salt
Olive oil spray
1 medium tomato, coarsely chopped
Several basil leaves, cut into bite-sized pieces
1 scallion, sliced
Salt and freshly ground black pepper

Mix chicken, pesto, black pepper, and salt together in a small bowl. Shape into burgers about 3½–4 inches in diameter and ½-inch thick. Heat a medium-sized nonstick skillet on medium-high heat. Spray with olive oil spray and sauté burgers 5 minutes on each side. Remove to 2 dinner plates.

Toss tomato, basil, and scallion together, and add salt and pepper to taste. Spoon over cooked burgers.

Makes 2 servings.

> Per serving: 381 calories, 56.6 grams protein, 7.0 grams carbohydrate, 15.0 grams fat (3.9 saturated), 149 milligrams cholesterol, 410 milligrams sodium, 0.8 grams fiber

warm mushroom salad

Olive oil spray
1/2 pound sliced portobello mushrooms
2 garlic cloves, crushed
Salt and freshly ground black pepper
2 tablespoons olive oil and vinegar dressing
Several radicchio leaves

Heat a nonstick skillet on medium-high heat and spray with olive oil. Add mushrooms and garlic. Sauté for 5 minutes. Add salt and pepper to taste. Remove to a small bowl. Add dressing and toss well. Place radicchio leaves on 2 dinner plates. Spoon mushrooms on to leaves.

Makes 2 servings.

> Per serving: 127 calories, 1.9 grams protein, 5.4 grams carbohydrate, 10.2 grams fat (1.6 saturated), 0 milligrams cholesterol, 80 milligrams sodium, 0.2 grams fiber

crab cakes and slaw

Crab cakes are very popular. Nearly every restaurant seems to have its own version, but the base usually has Worcestershire sauce, hot pepper sauce, and onions or scallions. Fresh crabmeat is best for this recipe. If difficult to find, use pasteurized crabmeat.

Homemade coleslaw is a breeze with a ready-to-eat, sliced coleslaw mix from the fruit and veg department.

crab cakes

1 pound fresh or pasteurized crabmeat

2 tablespoons reduced-fat mayonnaise

2 tablespoons Worcestershire sauce

Several drops hot pepper sauce

4 scallions, sliced

2 tablespoons Dijon mustard

2 egg whites

3 tablespoons plain breadcrumbs

Salt and freshly ground black pepper

2 tablespoons olive oil

Drain crabmeat. Flake meat with a fork while looking for any shell or cartilage that might remain. Mix the mayonnaise, Worcestershire sauce, hot pepper sauce, scallions, mustard, egg whites, and breadcrumbs together in a medium-sized bowl. Add salt and pepper to taste. Stir in crabmeat. Shape into 6 cakes about 3 inches in diameter. Heat olive oil in a medium-sized nonstick skillet on medium heat. Add crab cakes and cook for 5 minutes. Do not move crab cakes during this time. Carefully turn and cook for 5 minutes more. Serve crab cakes with coleslaw.
Makes 2 servings.

Per serving: 435 calories, 46.0 grams protein, 5.5 grams carbohydrate, 22.0 grams fat (3.4 saturated), 182 milligrams cholesterol, 1572 milligrams sodium, 0 grams fiber

slaw

2 tablespoons reduced-fat mayonnaise

1/4 cup distilled white vinegar

Sugar substitute equivalent to 2 teaspoons sugar

Salt and freshly ground black pepper

4 cups ready-to-eat coleslaw mix

Mix mayonnaise, vinegar, and sugar substitute together in a medium-sized bowl. Add salt and pepper to taste. Add coleslaw mix and toss well. Add more salt and pepper, if needed. Place on 2 plates.
Makes 2 servings.

Per serving: 94 calories, 2.0 grams protein, 11.1 grams carbohydrate, 5.4 grams fat (1.0 saturated), 5 milligrams cholesterol, 139 milligrams sodium, 2.0 grams fibre

helpful hints

● Frozen crabmeat can be used. The flavor will be fine; the texture will be softer than fresh crabmeat.

● Pasteurized crabmeat can be found in the seafood department.

● Different types of cabbage, ready-cut, can be found in the fruit and veg section of the supermarket. Use whichever you like.

countdown

● Make slaw.

● Make crab cakes.

shopping list

FRUIT AND VEG
   1 pack coleslaw mix
   1 small bunch scallions
SEAFOOD
   1 pound fresh or pasteurized crabmeat
GROCERY
   1 small container plain breadcrumbs
STAPLES
   Reduced-fat mayonnaise
   Worcestershire sauce
   Hot pepper sauce
   Dijon mustard
   Eggs (2 needed)
   Olive oil
   Distilled white vinegar
   Sugar substitute
   Salt
   Black peppercorns

helpful hints

- *Any type of green vegetable can be substituted for spinach.*
- *Look for shelled pistachio nuts in the supermarket.*

countdown

- *Make spinach and mushrooms.*
- *Make pork escalopes.*

shopping list

FRUIT AND VEG

2 medium tomatoes

1 (10-ounce) bag washed, ready-to-eat spinach

³/₄ pound sliced portobello mushrooms

MEAT

³/₄ pound pork fillet

GROCERY

1 small package shelled pistachio nuts

STAPLES

Olive oil

Garlic

Salt

Black peppercorns

pork escalopes with spinach and mushrooms

"Pork Escalopes with fresh sautéed tomatoes and garlic," was the instant answer a famous TV chef gave me when I asked her what she serves her family for a quick meal.

pork escalopes

¹/₂ pound pork tenderloins

2 tablespoons finely chopped pistachio nuts

Salt and freshly ground black pepper

1 teaspoon olive oil

2 medium garlic cloves, crushed

2 medium tomatoes, cut into 1-inch pieces

Remove fat from pork and cut into 1-inch slices. Place slices between 2 pieces of plastic wrap and flatten with the bottom of a heavy pan or a kitchen mallet. Place pistachio nuts on a plate and season with salt and pepper to taste. Press into pork on both sides. Heat oil in a large nonstick skillet on medium-high heat. Brown pork for 1 minute, then turn and brown second side for 1 minute. Salt and pepper the cooked sides. Remove to a plate. Add garlic and tomatoes to the pan and cook for 3 minutes. Spoon tomatoes over pork and serve.
Makes 2 servings.

> Per serving: 398 calories, 53.9 grams protein, 8.8 grams carbohydrate, 16.0 grams fat (3.9 saturated), 159 milligrams cholesterol, 126 milligrams sodium, 0 grams fiber

spinach and mushrooms

10 ounces washed, ready-to-eat spinach

³/₄ pound portobello mushrooms, sliced (4¹/₂ cups)

2 teaspoons olive oil

Salt and freshly ground black pepper

Place spinach and mushrooms in a large microwave-safe bowl. Microwave on high for 5 minutes. Remove and toss well. Add olive oil and salt and pepper to taste. Toss again.
Makes 2 servings.

> Per serving: 126 calories, 7.8 grams protein, 11.2 grams carbohydrate, 6.2 grams fat (0.6 saturated), 0 milligrams cholesterol, 174 milligrams sodium, 7.2 grams fiber

roasted salmon and herb sauce

Salmon, sprayed with a little olive oil and salt and pepper, takes on a buttery, creamy texture when roasted in a medium oven for 20 minutes. It is served with a herb sauce that takes only minutes in a food processor.

roasted salmon and herb sauce

2 x (6-ounce) salmon fillets
Olive oil spray
Salt and freshly ground black
   pepper
1 packed cup arugula
¼ cup nonfat plain yogurt
2 teaspoons fresh lemon or lime
   juice
1 tablespoon mayonnaise
1 medium tomato, sliced

Pre-heat oven to 350 degrees. Line a baking tray with foil. Place salmon on the tray and spray both sides of the fillet with olive oil spray. Sprinkle with salt and pepper to taste. Roast in oven for 20 minutes.

Meanwhile, remove any large stems from the arugula and place in a food processor. Add yoghurt, lemon juice, and mayonnaise. Process until smooth. Add salt and pepper to taste. Spoon over roasted salmon. Place sliced tomatoes on the side.
Makes 2 servings.

Per serving: 375 calories, 44.8 grams protein, 6.8 grams carbohydrate, 16.6 grams fat (3.5 saturated), 123 milligrams cholesterol, 180 milligrams sodium, 0 grams fiber

braised asparagus

³/₄ pound asparagus
½ cup water
1 teaspoon olive oil
Salt and freshly ground black
   pepper

Wash asparagus and cut about 1 inch off the woody ends. Place in a large nonstick skillet just large enough to hold them in one layer. Add the water, olive oil, and salt and pepper to taste. Bring to a simmer on medium-high heat and cover with lid. Lower heat to medium-low and cook for 10 minutes. Check the water halfway through the cooking and add more if the pan is dry. Serve with the salmon.
Makes 2 servings.

Per serving: 43 calories, 3 grams protein, 4.5 grams carbohydrate, 206 grams fat (0.4 saturated), 0 milligrams cholesterol, 138 milligrams sodium, 3.6 grams fiber

helpful hints

● *If you do not have a food processor, cut the arugula into small strips and mix with the other ingredients.*
● *If using thin asparagus, cut the braising time in half.*

countdown

● *Pre-heat oven to 350 degrees.*
● *Place salmon in oven.*
● *Make asparagus.*
● *While salmon and asparagus cook, make herb sauce.*

shopping list

FRUIT AND VEG
   ³/₄ pound asparagus
   1 bunch arugula (1½ ounces needed)
   1 medium tomato
DAIRY
   1 small carton nonfat plain yogurt (2 ounces needed)
SEAFOOD
   2 x (6-ounce) salmon fillets
STAPLES
   Olive oil
   Olive oil spray
   Lemon
   Mayonnaise
   Salt
   Black peppercorns

tuscan chicken

A fresh tomato-basil relish tops this simple chicken dish. The broccoli takes only minutes to cook in a microwave oven. It's topped with toasted almonds.

helpful hints

- *Any type of ripe tomato can be used for the relish.*
- *Fresh parsley or cilantro can be used instead of basil.*
- *A quick way to chop basil is to wash, dry and snip the leaves with scissors off the stem.*
- *To save washing an extra pan, sauté the almonds for a few minutes in a large skillet, then remove them and use the same pan to cook the chicken.*

countdown

- *Make tomato relish.*
- *Sauté almonds.*
- *Prepare chicken.*
- *Make broccoli.*

tuscan chicken

$1/2$ cup plum tomato, diced

2 tablespoons diced red onion

$1/4$ cup sliced sweet peppers, drained

$1/4$ cup snipped fresh basil leaves

$1/2$ tablespoon balsamic vinegar

Salt and freshly ground black pepper

$3/4$ pound boneless, skinless chicken breasts

Olive oil spray

Mix tomatoes, onion, sweet peppers, and basil together in a small bowl. Add vinegar and toss to mix. Add salt and pepper to taste. Set aside.

Place chicken between two pieces of greaseproof paper or foil and flatten with a kitchen mallet or the bottom of a heavy pan to $1/2$-inch thick.

Heat a large nonstick skillet on medium-high heat and spray with olive oil spray. Add chicken and sauté 3 minutes per side. Season to taste on the cooked sides. Divide between 2 dinner plates and spoon the tomato relish on top. *Makes 2 servings.*

Per serving: 307 calories, 54.6 grams protein, 4.2 grams carbohydrate, 9.0 grams fat (2.1 saturated), 144 milligrams cholesterol, 131 milligrams sodium, 0 grams fiber

toasted almond broccoli

4 tablespoons sliced almonds

1/2 pound broccoli florets

2 teaspoons olive oil

Salt and freshly ground black
pepper

Heat a nonstick skillet on medium heat and add the almonds. (This can be done in the same pan to be used for the chicken.) Sauté for 1 minute or until almonds are golden, not brown. Remove and set aside. Place broccoli in a microwave-safe bowl and microwave on high for 4 minutes. Remove and add oil and salt and pepper to taste. Toss well. Sprinkle almonds on top. *Makes 2 servings*.

Per serving: 213 calories, 9.7 grams protein, 13.4 grams carbohydrate, 16.2 grams fat (1.4 saturated), 0 milligrams cholesterol, 40 milligrams sodium, 4.9 grams fiber

shopping list

FRUIT AND VEG

1 large plum tomato

1 small bunch basil

1/2 pound broccoli florets

MEAT

3/4 pound boneless, skinless chicken breasts

GROCERY

1 small jar sweet peppers

1 1/2 ounces flaked almonds

STAPLES

Red onion

Olive oil spray

Olive oil

Balsamic vinegar

Salt

Black peppercorns

which carbs

When I teach classes, I find that this is the most important section. My students are afraid to start reintroducing carbs for fear they will negate all of the benefits they've achieved. Here's how you can prevent gaining lost weight.

The question that keeps coming up at every class is, "How do I start to add carbohydrates to my meals?" Two things usually happen at this point. You are losing weight and feeling good, so you stay on the Quick Start phase until you get bored or have a special event. Or you think, "Great. I've lost weight and now I can have the foods I love and forget about the carb restrictions." But neither solution leads to a healthy lifestyle of good-carb eating.

This section shows you how to start bringing carbs back into your life without gaining weight. I have carefully chosen these recipes to reincorporate high-fiber, low-simple-sugar carbohydrates.

The most important addition in this section is high-fiber cereal in the morning.

As with the other sections, I have organized the menus into a meal-at-a-glance chart incorporating some easy and quick meals from the Super Speed Supper section to accommodate busy mid-week schedules and some more elaborate recipes from the Weekend section suited to a more relaxed weekend pace. They are arranged to give variety throughout the day and over the days of the week.

Breakfast

You can choose from a variety of breakfasts to suit your taste. Quick ideas like microwave Ham-Baked Egg can be done in about 5 minutes. You can also enjoy an Italian Omelette.

Lunch

Cajun Shrimp Salad and a quick Horseradish-Crusted Salmon Salad are two of the tempting choices.

Dinner

Five-Spice Tuna Tataki and Veal Piccata are two of the meals that have been carefully planned to slowly reintroduce carbohydrates.

For those days when you are really pressed for time, select Peasant Country Soup and Swordfish in Spanish Sofrito Sauce from the Super Speed Suppers section of the book.

For weekends when you have more time and want something special, try the Steak in Port Wine or Chicken and Walnuts in Lettuce Puffs from the Weekends section of the book.

During the Which Carb 14-Day Meal Plan, which includes the Super Speed Suppers and Weekends meals, you will consume an average of 85–95 grams of carbohydrates per day. Carbohydrate percentage is based on carbohydrates less fiber consumed, which is the normal way of calculating carbohydrate consumption. The balance of these meals is 26 percent of calories from carbohydrates, 35 percent of calories from low-fat protein, 24 percent of calories from mono-unsaturated fat, and 10 percent of calories from saturated fat.

which carbs 14-day meal plan at a glance

week 1	breakfast	lunch	dinner
sunday	Tomato, Cheese, and Parsley Frittata 61	Italian Croque Monsieur 69	Mediterranean Snapper with Provençal Salad........................150
monday	Roast Beef and Cucumber Slices 62	Vietnamese Crab Soup 70	Crispy Mahi Mahi with Ratatouille................77
tuesday	Sausage Scramble 63	Cajun Shrimp Salad 71	Eggplant Parmesan with Linguine...................79
wednesday	Ginger-Cranberry Smoothie with Smoked Ham and Cheese........................64	Roast Chicken Vegetable Soup 72	Swordfish in Spanish Sofrito Sauce 131
thursday	Ham-Baked Egg 65	Rainbow Tomato Plate 73	Mediterranean Steak 80
friday	Italian Omelette 66	Horseradish-Crusted Salmon Salad..............74	Quick-Fried Diced Veal with Snow Peas and Rice......82
saturday	New Orleans Shrimp Roll 67	Chinese Chicken Salad..........................75	Adobo-Rubbed Cowboy Steak with Jalapeno rice.......................149

week 2	**breakfast**	**lunch**	**dinner**
sunday	Tomato Frittata 61	Italian Croque Monsieur...................69	Chicken and Walnuts in Lettuce Puffs...........152
monday	Roast Beef and Cucumber Slices 62	Vietnamese Crab Soup 70	Peasant Country Soup 132
tuesday	Sausage Scramble 63	Cajun Shrimp Salad 71	Beef Teriyaki with Chinese Noodles.................133
wednesday	Ginger-Cranberry Smoothie with Smoked Ham and Cheese 64	Roast Chicken Vegetable Soup 72	Five-Spice Tuna Tataki 84
thursday	Ham-Baked Egg 65	Rainbow Tomato Plate 73	Chicken with Black Bean Salsa Salad.........86
friday	Italian Omelette........... 66	Horseradish-Crusted Salmon Salad 74	Veal Piccata 88
saturday	New Orleans Shrimp Roll................. 67	Chinese Chicken Salad...................75	Steak in Port Wine....................154

which carbs
breakfasts

tomato, cheese and parsley frittata

Frittatas take about 10 minutes to make. They can be made ahead and eaten at room temperature.

A frittata needs to be cooked on both sides. Some people flip it in the pan. A much easier way is to place it in the oven to finish cooking, under a broiler for half a minute, or use this method of covering the frittata with a lid.

tomato frittata

2 whole eggs

6 egg whites

1 medium tomato, cut into 1-inch pieces

1 teaspoon dried thyme

1 cup fresh parsley, torn into bite-sized pieces

Salt and freshly ground black pepper

Olive oil spray

6 tablespoons grated part-skim milk mozzarella cheese

Lightly beat whole eggs and egg whites together. Add tomato, thyme, parsley, and salt and pepper to taste. Heat an 8–9-inch nonstick skillet over medium heat and spray with olive oil spray. Pour egg mixture into skillet. Spread to cover pan. Leave to set on the bottom for 1 minute. Sprinkle cheese on top. Turn heat to low, cover with a lid, and leave to cook for 10 minutes or until set. Cut in half and serve on 2 plates.

Makes 2 servings.

bran cereal

1 cup skim milk

1 cup high-fiber, no-sugar-added bran cereal

Divide between 2 cereal bowls.

Makes 2 servings.

Per serving: 324 calories, 32.8 grams protein, 36.3 grams carbohydrate, 12.9 grams fat (4.9 saturated), 231 milligrams cholesterol, 575 milligrams sodium, 13.0 grams fiber

helpful hints

- *Dried thyme is used in this recipe. Replace dried herbs after 6 months. If they look grey and old, that's probably how they will taste.*

countdown

- *Start frittata.*
- *While frittata cooks, assemble cereal.*
- *Finish frittata.*

shopping list

FRUIT AND VEG

1 medium tomato

1 small bunch parsley

DAIRY

1 small package part-skim milk mozzarella cheese

STAPLES

Dried thyme

Eggs (8 needed)

Skim milk

Olive oil spray

High-fiber, no-sugar-added bran cereal

Salt

Black peppercorns

roast beef and cucumber slices

This is a perfect breakfast to eat on the run. The roast beef slices can be made the night before and refrigerated.

roast beef and cucumber slices

1 medium cucumber
2 tablespoons reduced-fat
   mayonnaise
Salt and freshly ground black
   pepper
$1/2$ pound sliced, lean roast beef

Peel cucumber and slice about $1/4$-inch thick on the diagonal. Spread mayonnaise on each slice. Sprinkle with salt and pepper to taste. Fold the sliced roast beef to fit the cucumber slices and place on top. Divide between 2 plates.
Makes 2 servings.

helpful hints

- *Try to cut the cucumber slices on the diagonal. Hold the knife at an angle to the cucumber rather than perpendicular to it. This will give more surface area for the roast beef.*

countdown

- *Assemble the roast beef slices.*
- *Assemble cereal.*

shopping list

FRUIT AND VEG
   1 medium cucumber
DELI
   $1/2$ pound sliced, lean
      roast beef
STAPLES
   Skim milk
   High-fiber, no-sugar-added
      bran cereal
   Reduced-fat mayonnaise
   Salt
   Black peppercorns

sausage scramble

Lean, mild turkey sausage makes these scrambled eggs special. If your local butcher makes his own sausages you may be able to get spicy or special herbed versions. Choose whichever you like.

sausage scramble

6 ounces mild, low-fat turkey
  sausages, cut into 1/2 inch slices
2 whole eggs
4 egg whites
1/2 teaspoon dried oregano
Salt and freshly ground black
  pepper

Heat a medium-sized nonstick skillet on medium-high heat. Add sausage slices and cook for 3 minutes. While sausage cooks, mix whole eggs and whites together and add oregano and salt and pepper to taste. Add egg mixture to the skillet. Scramble for 1 minute, or until egg is cooked to desired doneness.
Makes 2 servings.

oatmeal

1 cup oatmeal
2 cups water
1 cup skim milk
1 teaspoon cinnamon
Sugar substitute equivalent to
  2 teaspoons sugar

To prepare in the microwave, combine oatmeal and water together. Microwave on high for 4 minutes. Stir in milk, cinnamon, and sugar substitute. Alternatively, combine oatmeal and water in a small saucepan. Bring to the boil. Cook about 5 minutes over medium heat, stirring occasionally. Stir in milk, cinnamon, and sugar substitute.
Makes 2 servings.

Per serving: 442 calories, 37.3 grams protein, 37.6 grams carbohydrate, 16.9 grams fat (4.3 saturated), 260 milligrams cholesterol, 777 milligrams sodium, 4.2 grams fiber

helpful hints

● *Dried oregano is used in this recipe. Replace dried herbs after 6 months. If they look grey and old, that's probably how they will taste.*

countdown

● *Make oatmeal.*
● *Make sausage scramble.*

shopping list

MEAT
  6 ounces low-fat turkey
    sausages
STAPLES
  Dried oregano
  Eggs (6 needed)
  Oatmeal
  Skim milk
  Cinnamon
  Sugar substitute
  Salt
  Black peppercorns

ginger-cranberry smoothie with smoked ham and cheese

Ginger gives this colorful smoothie an Oriental taste.

ginger-cranberry smoothie

1/4 cup fresh or frozen cranberries
1/4 cup water
1/2 cup nonfat vanilla yogurt
1 teaspoon ground ginger
Sugar substitute equivalent to
    4 teaspoons sugar
2 cups ice cubes

Place cranberries, water, yogurt, ginger, and sugar substitute in a blender. Blend until smooth. Add the ice cubes and blend until thick. Pour into 2 glasses.
Makes 2 servings.

smoked ham and cheese

Several lettuce leaves
1/2 pound smoked, lean ham, cut
    into 1/2-inch cubes
2 ounces reduced-fat Cheddar
    cheese, torn into bite-sized
    pieces

Place lettuce on 2 plates with ham and cheese sprinkled on top.
Makes 2 servings.

bran cereal

1 cup skim milk
1 cup high-fiber, no-sugar-added
    bran cereal

Divide between 2 cereal bowls.
Makes 2 servings.

Per serving: 394 calories, 38.4 grams protein, 42.6 grams carbohydrate, 13.1 grams fat (6.2 saturated), 76 milligrams cholesterol, 1473 milligrams sodium, 14.2 grams fiber

ham-baked egg

Baked or shirred eggs are easy to make and are a nice change. They take about 12–15 minutes in the oven. I've shortened the time to 2 minutes by "baking" them in a microwave oven. The secret is to gently prick the egg yolk in 2 places to break the membrane before placing in the microwave.

ham-baked egg

2 teaspoons olive oil
1/2 pound lean ham torn into bite-
    sized pieces
2 whole eggs
Salt and freshly ground black
    pepper

Spoon oil into 2 small ramekins. Divide ham into 2 portions and place in the ramekins. Break 1 egg into each dish. With the tip of a very sharp knife make 2 tiny pricks in each egg yolk, just to break the membrane and let steam escape. Sprinkle with salt and pepper to taste. Place one ramekin in a microwave oven. Cover ramekin with a piece of kitchen paper and microwave on high for 1 minute. Remove and serve. Repeat with second ramekin.
Makes 2 servings.

oatmeal

1 cup oatmeal
2 cups water
1 cup skim milk
Sugar substitute equivalent to
    2 teaspoons sugar

To prepare in the microwave, combine oatmeal and water together. Microwave on high for 4 minutes. Stir in milk and sugar substitute. Alternatively, combine oatmeal and water in a small saucepan. Bring to the boil. Cook about 5 minutes over medium heat, stirring occasionally. Stir in milk and sugar substitute.
Makes 2 servings.

Per serving: 458 calories, 37.2 grams protein, 35.7 grams carbohydrate, 19.1 grams fat (4.9 saturated), 268 milligrams cholesterol, 1110 milligrams sodium, 4 grams fiber

helpful hints

● *Cook the eggs for 1 1/2 minutes (3 minutes total) for a firmer yolk.*
● *Small dessert or glass bowls can be used instead of ramekins. They should measure about 3–4 inches wide and 2 inches deep.*

countdown

● *Assemble eggs and ham in ramekins.*
● *Assemble cereal.*
● *Microwave eggs.*

shopping list

DELI
    1/2 pound lean, smoked ham
STAPLES
    Eggs (2 needed)
    Skim milk
    Olive oil
    Oatmeal
    Salt
    Black peppercorns
    Sugar substitute

italian omelette

A perfect omelette is golden on the top with a delicate creamy center. The secret is to cook it over medium-high heat for only a couple of minutes while gently scraping the side to make sure all of the egg is cooked.

helpful hints

- *Buy good-quality Parmesan cheese and grate it yourself or chop it in the food processor. Freeze extra for quick use. You can quickly spoon out what you need and leave the rest frozen.*

countdown

- *Prepare omelette ingredients.*
- *Assemble bran cereal.*
- *Make omelette.*

shopping list

DAIRY

  1 small carton ricotta cheese

GROCERY

  1 small jar low-sugar, low-fat chunky marinara sauce

STAPLES

  Egg substitute

  Parmesan cheese

  Skim milk

  Olive oil

  High-fiber, no-sugar-added bran cereal

  Black peppercorns

italian omelette

¼ cup nonfat ricotta cheese
¼ cup bottled low-sugar, low-fat chunky marinara sauce
¼ cup grated Parmesan cheese
1½ cups egg substitute
Freshly ground black pepper
2 teaspoons olive oil

Mix ricotta cheese, marinara sauce and Parmesan cheese together and set aside. Mix egg substitute with pepper to taste. Heat oil in a medium-sized nonstick skillet on medium-high heat. Pour in the egg mixture. Let the eggs set for about 30 seconds. Tip the pan and lightly move the eggs so that they all set. Spread the cheese mixture on half the omelette and fold the omelette in half. Slide out of the pan by tipping the pan and holding a plate vertically against the side of the pan. Turn the pan and plate to invert the omelette on to the plate. Cut in half and serve on 2 plates.
Makes 2 servings.

bran cereal

1 cup skim milk
1 cup high-fiber, no-sugar-added bran cereal

Divide between 2 cereal bowls.
Makes 2 servings.

365 calories, 32.6 grams protein, 36.8 grams carbohydrate, 12.4 grams fat (4.5 saturated), 17 milligrams cholesterol, 1076 milligrams sodium, 13.0 grams fiber

new orleans shrimp roll

Shrimp and hot pepper sauce give this roll-up a hint of New Orleans cooking. The egg is cooked like a crêpe and used as a wrap.

new orleans shrimp roll

½ pound cooked shrimp, peeled and deveined
2 tablespoons mayonnaise
Several drops hot pepper sauce
Salt and freshly ground black pepper
1 cup egg substitute
Olive oil spray

Coarsely chop the shrimp. Add mayonnaise and hot pepper sauce. Add salt and pepper to taste. Mix egg substitute with salt and pepper to taste.

Heat a medium-sized nonstick skillet on medium-high heat. Spray with olive oil spray and pour half the egg substitute into the pan and spread to make a thin layer. Leave to cook for 2 minutes. Turn over for 1 minute. Remove from heat. Spread half the shrimp mixture on top.

Roll up and place on a plate. Repeat for second serving.

Makes 2 servings.

oatmeal

1 cup oatmeal
2 cups water
1 cup skim milk
Sugar substitute equivalent to 2 teaspoons sugar

To prepare in the microwave, combine oatmeal and water together. Microwave on high for 4 minutes. Stir in milk and sugar substitute. Alternatively, combine oatmeal and water in a small saucepan. Bring to the boil. Cook for about 5 minutes over medium heat, stirring occasionally. Stir in milk and sugar substitute.

Makes 2 servings.

Per serving: 473 calories, 44.3 grams protein, 36.5 grams carbohydrate, 16.0 grams fat (2.6 saturated), 180 milligrams cholesterol, 535 milligrams sodium, 4 grams fiber

helpful hints

● *Cooked, shelled shrimp can be found in the fish department or frozen in most supermarkets.*
● *Use the pulse button on a food processor to coarsely chop the shrimp.*

countdown

● *Prepare shrimp filling.*
● *Make shrimp roll.*
● *Assemble cereal.*

shopping list

SEAFOOD
  ³/4 pound cooked, peeled, deveined shrimp
STAPLES
  Mayonnaise
  Egg substitute
  Olive oil spray
  Hot pepper sauce
  Skim milk
  Oatmeal
  Sugar substitute
  Salt
  Black peppercorns

which carbs
lunches

italian croque monsieur

Nearly every brasserie in Paris serves a version of croque monsieur (grilled ham and cheese sandwich). Here is an Italian version.

italian croque monsieur

Olive oil spray
4 slices wholemeal bread
¼ pound part-skim milk mozzarella cheese, sliced
½ pound lean ham, sliced
1 medium tomato, sliced
½ cup fresh basil, torn into bite-sized pieces (optional)

Pre-heat broiler. Line a baking tray with foil and spray with olive oil spray. Place bread on foil and spray bread. Place cheese and then ham on bread. Top with sliced tomato. Broil for 2 minutes or until cheese melts. Remove and sprinkle with basil.
Makes 2 servings.

Per serving: 424 calories, 44.7 grams protein, 26.3 grams carbohydrate, 18.9 grams fat (8.3 saturated), 86 milligrams cholesterol, 1483 milligrams sodium, 6.0 grams fiber

dessert

2 cups watermelon cubes

Divide between 2 small dessert dishes.
Makes 2 servings.

Per serving: 49 calories, 1.0 gram protein, 11.0 grams carbohydrate, 0.6 grams fat (0.1 saturated), 0 milligrams cholesterol, 3 milligrams sodium, 0.8 grams fiber

helpful hints

- *Watermelon cubes can be found in the fruit and veg section of some supermarkets.*

countdown

- *Pre-heat broiler.*
- *Make sandwich.*
- *While sandwich toasts, place watermelon in dishes.*

shopping list

FRUIT AND VEG
1 small bunch basil
1 medium tomato
1 small container watermelon cubes
DAIRY
1 small package part-skim milk mozzarella cheese
DELI
½ pound lean ham
STAPLES
Olive oil spray
Whole wheat bread

vietnamese crab soup

This soup is filled with the fragrant flavors of South-east Asia. As with most Asian dishes, it takes a little longer to prepare the ingredients, but then it takes less than 5 minutes to cook.

Lemongrass, which adds a special lemon flavor to Asian dishes, can be found in some supermarkets. It looks a bit like a scallion, but the stalks are a pale green color, hard and dry. Use the white bulbous end for the soup.

helpful hints

- If fresh crab is unavailable, use crab, or shrimp.
- One tablespoon lime juice can be substituted for the lemongrass.
- A quick way to chop ginger is to peel, dice, and press through a garlic press with large holes. The pulp will not go through but the juice is enough to flavor the dish.
- Cubed fresh honeydew melon can be bought in most supermarkets.

countdown

- Assemble soup ingredients.
- Place melon cubes in dessert dishes.
- Complete soup.

shopping list

FRUIT AND VEG

1 small bunch lemongrass
(2 stalks needed)

1 lime

5 ounces fresh snow peas

1 small bag bean sprouts

1 small bunch scallions

1 small container fresh honeydew melon cubes

1 small piece fresh ginger

SEAFOOD

3/4 pound fresh or pasteurized crabmeat

GROCERY

1 small bottle sesame oil

STAPLES

Fat-free, low-sodium chicken broth

Hot pepper sauce

vietnamese crab soup

2 cups fat-free, low-sodium chicken broth

2 cups water

2 stalks lemongrass, tender white base only, sliced

1 tablespoon peeled and coarsely chopped fresh ginger

1 tablespoon lime zest

5 ounces fresh snow peas, trimmed

1 cup bean sprouts

3/4 pound fresh or pasteurized crabmeat, drained

2 tablespoons sesame oil

Several drops hot pepper sauce

Salt and freshly ground black pepper

2 scallions, sliced

Place chicken broth and water in a large saucepan. Add lemongrass, ginger, lime zest, and snow peas. Bring to a simmer on medium heat and cook for 2 minutes. Add bean sprouts and crab. Simmer for 2 more minutes. Remove from heat and add hot pepper sauce, sesame oil, and salt and pepper to taste. Ladle into 2 soup bowls and sprinkle scallions on top.
Makes 2 servings.

Per serving: 343 calories, 37.3 grams protein, 11.8 grams carbohydrate, 15.8 grams fat (2.2 saturated), 133 milligrams cholesterol, 1070 milligrams sodium, 2.6 grams fiber

dessert

2 cups honeydew melon cubes

Divide between 2 small dessert plates.
Makes 2 servings.

Per serving: 57 calories, 1.4 grams protein, 13.4 grams carbohydrate, 0.4 grams fat (0 saturated), 0 milligrams cholesterol, 14 milligrams sodium, 0.5 grams fiber

cajun shrimp salad

The hot spices of Louisiana Cajun country flavor this quick shrimp salad.

cajun shrimp salad

2 tablespoons no-sugar-added oil and vinegar dressing

2 garlic cloves, crushed

1/2 teaspoon cayenne

1 teaspoon dried oregano

1 teaspoon dried thyme

3/4 pound cooked shrimp, peeled, deveined, and cut in half

1 small head cos lettuce heart

1 medium red bell pepper, cut into small cubes

In a small bowl, mix dressing with garlic, cayenne, oregano, and thyme. Add shrimp and toss well. Tear lettuce into bite-sized pieces and place on 2 plates. Mix red bell pepper with shrimp and spoon shrimp and dressing over lettuce.
Makes 2 servings.

Per serving: 301 calories, 37.2 grams protein, 10.6 grams carbohydrate, 11.7 grams fat (1.9 saturated), 260 milligrams cholesterol, 342 milligrams sodium, 0.9 grams fiber

dessert

2 oranges

Divide between 2 small plates.
Makes 2 servings.

Per serving: 62 calories, 1.2 grams protein, 15.4 grams carbohydrate, 0.2 grams fat (0 saturated), 0 milligrams cholesterol, 0 milligrams sodium, 3.1 grams fiber

helpful hints

- *Cooked, shelled shrimp can be found in the fish department or frozen in the frozen section of most supermarkets.*
- *Prepared Cajun spice mix can be used instead of the spice mixture in the recipe. Make sure no sugar or salt is added to the mixture.*
- *Dried oregano, thyme, and cayenne pepper are used in this recipe. Replace dried herbs after 6 months. If they look grey and old, that's probably how they will taste.*

countdown

- *Make dressing.*
- *Complete salad.*

shopping list

FRUIT AND VEG

1 small head cos lettuce heart

1 medium red bell pepper

2 oranges

SEAFOOD

3/4 pound cooked, peeled, and deveined shrimp

STAPLES

Dried thyme

Dried oregano

Cayenne pepper

No-sugar-added oil and vinegar dressing

Garlic

roast chicken vegetable soup

A cheery bowl of soup is a treat any time of year. This soup uses roasted, ready-to-eat chicken and can be ready in less than 15 minutes. The soup tastes great the second day. Make extra if you have time and save for a second day or freeze.

helpful hints

- *Any type of mushroom can be used.*
- *Buy good-quality Parmesan cheese and grate it yourself or chop it in the food processor. Freeze extra for quick use. You can quickly spoon out what you need and leave the rest frozen.*
- *Fresh pineapple cubes can be found in the fruit and veg section of most supermarkets.*

countdown

- *Start soup.*
- *While soup cooks, assemble pineapple dessert.*
- *Complete soup.*

shopping list

FRUIT AND VEG
½ pound mushrooms
1 small bunch thyme or dried thyme
1 small container fresh pineapple cubes
MEAT
½ pound roasted, ready-to-eat chicken pieces
STAPLES
Yellow onion
Celery
Fat-free, low-sodium chicken broth
Parmesan cheese
Olive oil
Salt
Black peppercorns

roast chicken vegetable soup

2 teaspoons olive oil
½ cup sliced yellow onion
1 celery stalk, sliced
½ pound mushrooms, sliced
2 cups fat-free, low-sodium chicken broth
1 cup water
2 large sprigs fresh thyme or 1 teaspoon dried thyme
½ pound roasted, ready-to-eat chicken pieces
Salt and freshly ground black pepper
2 tablespoons grated Parmesan cheese

Heat oil in a large saucepan over medium-high heat and add onion and celery. Sauté for 3 minutes. Add mushrooms, broth, water, and thyme. Reduce heat to medium and simmer for 7 minutes. Add chicken and cook for 2 minutes or until chicken is warmed through. Remove thyme sprigs and add salt and pepper to taste. Spoon into 2 soup bowls and sprinkle Parmesan on top.
Makes 2 servings.

Per serving: 334 calories, 44.8 grams protein, 8.3 grams carbohydrate, 13.5 grams fat (3.6 saturated), 103 milligrams cholesterol, 858 milligrams sodium, 0.5 grams fiber

dessert

2 cups pineapple cubes

Divide between 2 dessert dishes.
Makes 2 servings.

Per serving: 77 calories, 0.6 grams protein, 19.2 grams carbohydrate, 0.7 grams fat (0 saturated), 0 milligrams cholesterol, 1 milligram sodium, 2.4 grams fiber

rainbow tomato plate

This colorful salad plate accented with red and yellow tomatoes takes only 5 minutes to assemble.

rainbow tomato plate

2 small red tomatoes, sliced

2 small yellow tomatoes, sliced

1 medium cucumber, peeled and sliced

¼ cup pinenuts

6 ounces smoked chicken breast, cut into cubes

2 tablespoons no-sugar-added oil and vinegar dressing

Salt and freshly ground black pepper

Arrange the sliced tomatoes and cucumber in circles on 2 plates, alternating red tomato slices, yellow tomato slices, and cucumber slices. The slices should cover the plate. Sprinkle chicken cubes and pinenuts over tomatoes. Drizzle dressing over the top. Sprinkle with salt and pepper to taste.

Makes 2 servings.

Per serving: 354 calories, 32.1 grams protein, 15.1 grams carbohydrate, 13.0 grams fat (2.2 saturated), 72 milligrams cholesterol, 161 milligrams sodium, 0.9 grams fiber

dessert

1 cup light fruit yogurt

Divide yogurt between 2 small dessert bowls.

Makes 2 servings.

Per serving: 70 calories, 5.5 grams protein, 11.5 grams carbohydrate, 0 grams fat (0 saturated), 3 milligrams cholesterol, 95 milligrams sodium, 0 grams fiber

helpful hints

- *Any type of tomatoes can be used.*
- *Any flavor light yogurt can be used for dessert.*
- *Extra pinenuts can be stored in the freezer.*

countdown

- *Make salad plate.*
- *Serve yogurt.*

shopping list

FRUIT AND VEG

2 small red tomatoes

2 small yellow tomatoes

1 medium cucumber

DAIRY

1 carton light fruit yogurt

DELI

6 ounces smoked chicken breast

GROCERY

1 small package pinenuts

STAPLES

No-sugar-added oil and vinegar dressing

Salt

Black peppercorns

horseradish-crusted salmon salad

A spicy, creamy crust covers the rich salmon fillet for this quick lunch. The salmon tastes great served either hot or at room temperature.

horseradish-crusted salmon salad

Olive oil spray
1/2 pound salmon fillet
Salt and freshly ground black
    pepper
2 tablespoons prepared
    horseradish
2 tablespoons mayonnaise
4 cups washed, ready-to-eat
    romaine lettuce leaves
1 medium cucumber, peeled and
    sliced

Pre-heat broiler. Line a baking tray with foil and spray with olive oil spray. Place salmon on the tray. Sprinkle with salt and pepper to taste. Broil for 3 minutes. Mix horseradish and mayonnaise together. Remove salmon and turn over. Spread with horseradish mixture. Return to broiler for 3 minutes. Place lettuce and cucumber on 2 plates. Remove salmon and divide in half. Place over salad.
Makes 2 servings.

> Per serving: 340 calories, 30.4 grams protein, 8.7 grams carbohydrate, 19.3 grams fat (3.4 saturated), 85 milligrams cholesterol, 181 milligrams sodium, 1.5 grams fiber

dessert

2 medium apples

Serve 1 apple per person.
Makes 2 servings.

> Per serving: 81 calories, 0.3 grams protein, 21.1 grams carbohydrate, 0.5 grams fat (0.1 saturated), 0 milligrams cholesterol, 0 milligrams sodium, 3.7 grams fiber

helpful hints

● *The salmon keeps well and can be served the next day. Make double the portion for another quick lunch.*

countdown

● *Pre-heat broiler.*
● *Make salmon.*
● *While salmon cooks, prepare lettuce and cucumber.*

shopping list

FRUIT AND VEG
    1 bag washed, ready-to-eat
        cos lettuce leaves
    1 medium cucumber
    2 medium apples
SEAFOOD
    1/2 pound salmon fillet
GROCERY
    1 small jar prepared
        horseradish
STAPLES
    Olive oil spray
    Mayonnaise
    Salt
    Black peppercorns

chinese chicken salad

Adding Chinese five-spice powder and soy sauce to a bottled oil and vinegar dressing gives this salad an aromatic Chinese flavor.

chinese chicken salad

1 tablespoon low-sodium soy
　sauce

½ teaspoon five-spice powder

2 tablespoons no-sugar-added oil
　and vinegar dressing

1 cup bean sprouts

½ pound roasted, ready-to-eat
　chicken pieces

Salt and freshly ground black
　pepper

3 cups sliced Chinese cabbage

4 tangerines, peeled and
　segmented

In a medium-sized bowl, mix soy sauce, five-spice powder and dressing together. Add the bean sprouts and chicken and toss well. Add salt and pepper to taste. Place cabbage on 2 plates and spoon chicken mixture on top. Sprinkle tangerine segments on top.

Makes 2 servings.

Per serving: 388 calories, 40.6 grams protein,
28.9 grams carbohydrate, 14.5 grams fat
(2.5 saturated), 96 milligrams cholesterol,
485 milligrams sodium, 2.4 grams fiber

helpful hints

● *Chinese cabbage is also called Chinese leaves.*
● *Any type of lettuce can be used.*

countdown

● *Mix dressing ingredients together.*
● *Complete salad.*
● *Assemble dessert.*

shopping list

FRUIT AND VEG
　*1 small Chinese cabbage
　　(Chinese leaves)*
　*1 small package fresh bean
　　sprouts*
　4 tangerines
MEAT
　*½ pound roasted, ready-to-
　　eat chicken pieces*
GROCERY
　1 small jar five-spice powder
STAPLES
　Low-sodium soy sauce
　*No-sugar-added oil and
　　vinegar dressing*
　Salt
　Black peppercorns

which carbs

dinners

crispy mahi mahi with ratatouille

For this quick meal, freshly made ratatouille, a tasty blend of Provençal vegetables, is combined with juicy fish fillets. Coating the fish fillet with polenta gives it a crispy crust without having to deep-fry it.

I am often asked how to cook fish so that it's juicy and not dried out. The general rule is to cook fish for 10 minutes for each 1 inch of thickness. If the fish is thicker, cook it a little longer, or if thinner, cook it a shorter time.

crispy mahi mahi

³/₄ pound mahi mahi fillet
2 tablespoons coarse cornmeal
Salt and freshly ground black pepper
2 teaspoons olive oil

Wash fish fillet and pat dry with kitchen paper. Season polenta with salt and pepper to taste. Dip fish into polenta, making sure both sides are well coated. Heat olive oil in a medium-sized nonstick skillet on medium-high heat. Add fish and sauté for 5 minutes. Turn and sauté another 5 minutes for a 1-inch thick fillet. Reduce cooking time to 8 total minutes for ¹/₂-inch fillet. Divide in half and serve.

Makes 2 servings.

> Per serving: 203 calories, 29.3 grams protein, 5.6 grams carbohydrate, 6.0 grams fat (1.0 saturated), 116 milligrams cholesterol, 136 milligrams sodium, 0 grams fiber

ratatouille (sautéed Provençal vegetables)

6 ounces eggplant, washed and sliced
6 ounces zucchinis, washed and sliced
¹/₂ cup sliced red onion
2 medium garlic cloves, crushed
2 cups low-sodium, low-sugar tomato or pasta sauce
¹/₂ cup water
2 teaspoons olive oil
Salt and freshly ground black pepper

Add eggplant, zucchinis, onion, garlic, tomato sauce, and water to a medium-sized saucepan. Bring to a simmer over medium-high heat. Lower heat and cover. Simmer for 15 minutes. Vegetables should be cooked through but a little firm. Stir in olive oil and add salt and pepper to taste.

Makes 2 servings.

> Per serving: 223 calories, 5.9 grams protein, 18.9 grams carbohydrate, 4.7 grams fat (0.6 saturated), 0 milligrams cholesterol, 44 milligrams sodium, 3.5 grams fiber

helpful hints

- *You can use haddock, bass, or grouper in place of the mahi mahi.*
- *For the pumpkin pudding, use the mixture of spices given or use a mixed spice mixture, making sure no sugar has been added.*

countdown

- *Start ratatouille.*
- *Make pumpkin pudding.*
- *Prepare fish.*

shopping list

FRUIT AND VEG
  6 ounces eggplant
  6 ounces zucchinis
DAIRY
  1 carton nonfat vanilla yogurt
SEAFOOD
  ³/₄ pound mahi mahi fillets
GROCERY
  1 small package polenta
  1 small can 100% pure
    pumpkin
  1 small package pecan pieces
STAPLES:
  Red onion
  Garlic
  Olive oil
  Low-sodium, low-sugar
    tomato or pasta sauce
  Sugar substitute
  Ground cinnamon
  Grated nutmeg
  Salt
  Black peppercorns

crispy mahi mahi with ratatouille
continued

pumpkin pudding

³/₄ cup canned 100% pure
  pumpkin
³/₄ cup nonfat vanilla yogurt
¹/₈ teaspoon ground cinnamon
¹/₈ teaspoon grated nutmeg
Sugar substitute equivalent to
  2 teaspoons sugar
2 tablespoons pecan pieces

Mix together pumpkin, cinnamon, nutmeg, and sugar substitute. Fold into yogurt. Toast pecan pieces in the oven or under a broiler until golden, about 2 minutes. Divide pumpkin mixture between 2 small dessert bowls or ramekins and sprinkle pecans on top. *Makes 2 servings.*

Per serving: 162 calories, 6.2 grams protein, 18.4 grams carbohydrate, 8.4 grams fat (0.9 saturated), 2 milligrams cholesterol, 73 milligrams sodium, 3.7 grams fiber

eggplant parmesan with linguine

Eggplant parmesan, my husband's favourite dish, is a Neapolitan dish made with slices of fried eggplant baked in a rich tomato sauce and Parmesan cheese. I've created this quick version by microwaving the slices instead. It also makes the dish much lighter, as fried eggplant soaks up a lot of oil during the cooking.

eggplant parmesan with linguine

Olive oil spray

1/2 pound eggplant, cut into
   1/4-inch slices

Salt and freshly ground black
   pepper

1 1/2 cups low-sodium, no-sugar-
   added, tomato sauce

6 ounces lean ground beef

1 cup arugula leaves

1/2 cup part-skim milk ricotta
   cheese

3 tablespoons water

3 tablespoons grated Parmesan
   cheese

1/4 pound whole wheat linguine

2 teaspoons olive oil

Pre-heat the broiler. Bring a large saucepan filled with 3–4 quarts of water to the boil. Arrange eggplant slices on a 9–10 inch microwave-safe pie dish. Spray with olive oil and sprinkle with salt and pepper to taste. Cover with plastic wrap or a plate. Microwave on high for 3 minutes. Carefully remove cover. Remove eggplant to a plate and set aside.

Mix tomato sauce and minced beef together in a microwave-safe bowl. Microwave on high for 3 minutes. Spoon a layer of meat sauce into the bottom of the pie dish. Place arugula leaves over sauce. Place a layer of eggplant slices over the sauce and sprinkle with a little salt and pepper to taste. Repeat with the sauce, eggplant, and salt and pepper.

Mix ricotta cheese with water to form a sauce consistency. Add more water if necessary. Spoon ricotta cheese over top of eggplant dish. Sprinkle with Parmesan cheese. Broil for 5 minutes until sauce is bubbly and cheese melted. Place linguine in boiling water for 9 minutes. Drain and toss with olive oil and add salt and pepper to taste.

Place linguine on 2 dinner plates and serve eggplant parmesan on top. *Makes 2 servings.*

Per serving: 597 calories, 53.3 grams protein, 50.1 grams carbohydrate, 19.1 grams fat (10.1 saturated), 122 milligrams cholesterol, 446 milligrams sodium, 9.1 grams fiber

helpful hints

● *Buy Parmesan cheese and grate it yourself or chop it in a food processor. Freeze extra for quick use. You can spoon out what you need and leave the rest frozen.*

● *This dish can be prepared and assembled in advance and refrigerated several hours or overnight. Bring to room temperature and broiler as needed.*

countdown

● *Pre-heat broiler.*
● *Boil water for pasta.*
● *Microwave eggplant.*
● *Mix ricotta.*
● *Assemble eggplant parmesan and place under broiler.*
● *Boil linguine.*

shopping list

FRUIT AND VEG
   1/2 pound eggplant
   1 small bunch arugula
DAIRY
   1 small carton low-fat ricotta
      cheese
MEAT
   6 ounces lean ground beef
GROCERY
   1 small package whole wheat
      linguine (2 ounces
      needed)
STAPLES
   Parmesan cheese
   Olive oil
   Low-sodium, no-sugar-
      added tomato sauce
      (12 ounces needed)
   Salt
   Black peppercorns

mediterranean steak

helpful hints

● *Use a skillet that just fits the steak to capture the pan juices. A larger pan will cause the juices to boil away.*
● *Buy sliced olives.*

countdown

● *Bring water for couscous to the boil.*
● *Prepare ingredients for steak.*
● *Make couscous.*
● *Finish steak.*

Sautéed steak flavored with the bountiful produce of the Mediterranean provides a quick, 15-minute dinner.

Pre-cooked, packaged couscous takes only 5 minutes to make. It's made from semolina flour and is in fact a form of pasta rather than a grain as many people think. You just boil water, remove from heat, add the couscous, cover, and leave to stand. For this dinner, I've added fresh mint and chopped tomatoes to add a fresh flavor that goes well with the steak.

mediterranean steak

³/₄ pound steak (strip, flank, or skirt)
¹/₄ teaspoon cayenne pepper
Olive oil spray
3 tablespoons sliced pimiento-stuffed green olives
2 tablespoons capers
Salt and freshly ground black pepper

Remove fat from steak and sprinkle both sides with cayenne. Heat a small, nonstick skillet over medium-high heat. Spray with olive oil spray. Brown steak for 2 minutes per side. Sprinkle olives and capers into skillet and over steak. Lower heat to medium and cook 2 minutes for medium-rare. Cook 2 minutes longer for thick steak. Add salt and pepper to taste.

To serve, place couscous on 2 dinner plates, carve steak, and place on top. Spoon any pan juices over steak.
Makes 2 servings.

Per serving: 356 calories, 55.8 grams protein, 0.3 grams carbohydrate, 16.4 grams fat (7.1 saturated), 140 milligrams cholesterol, 548 milligrams sodium, 0 grams fiber

minted couscous

¹/₂ cup water
¹/₃ cup couscous
1 small tomato, diced
3 cups cucumber, cut into cubes
¹/₄ cup chopped fresh mint
Salt and freshly ground black pepper

Bring water to the boil. Remove from heat and add couscous, tomatoes, and cucumber. Cover with a lid and leave to stand for 5 minutes. When ready, fluff with a fork. Add mint and salt and pepper to taste.
Makes 2 servings.

Per serving: 144 calories, 5.9 grams protein, 30.0 grams carbohydrate, 0.9 grams fat (0 saturated), 0 milligrams cholesterol, 11 milligrams sodium, 1.9 grams fiber

Crispy Mahi Mahi with Ratatouille   **p77–8**

spiced peaches

2 medium peaches, pitted and
    sliced
1/2 teaspoon ground cinnamon
1/4 teaspoon allspice
Sugar substitute equivalent to
    1 teaspoon sugar
2 sprigs fresh mint

Arrange peach slices in a circle on 2 small dessert plates. Mix cinnamon, allspice, and sugar substitute together. Sprinkle mixture over peach slices. Place both dishes in a microwave oven on high for 1 minute. Remove, garnish with mint leaves, and serve.
Makes 2 servings.

Per serving: 39 calories, 0.6 grams protein, 10.7 grams carbohydrate, 0.1 gram fat (0 saturated), 0 milligrams cholesterol, 0 milligrams sodium, 0.5 grams fiber

shopping list

FRUIT AND VEG
    1 small bunch fresh mint
    1 small tomato
    2 medium peaches
    1 small cucumber
MEAT
    3/4 pound steak (strip, flank,
        or skirt)
GROCERY
    1 small package couscous
    1 small jar/can pimiento-
        stuffed green olives
    1 small jar capers
    1 small jar allspice
STAPLES
    Olive oil spray
    Cayenne pepper
    Ground cinnamon
    Sugar substitute
    Salt
    Black peppercorns

quick-fried diced veal

A stir-fry dish with a mystery flavor makes a delicious, quick dinner. The grapefruit nearly melts away leaving an intriguing flavor and texture.

Stir-fry dishes take a little extra time to prepare the ingredients, but take only a few minutes to cook. I find it is best to line up all of the stir-fry ingredients on a plate or chopping board in order of use. You won't have to keep referring to the recipe while cooking.

Brown rice takes about 45 minutes to cook. There are several brands of quick-cooking brown rice available. Their cooking time ranges from 10 to 30 minutes. I find the 30-minute rice has more flavor, but any quick-cooking brown rice will work for this dinner.

helpful hints

- *Your wok or skillet should be very hot so the veal will be crisp, not steamed.*
- *Peel and segment grapefruit over a bowl to catch the juice. This will give you the 2 tablespoons of grapefruit juice needed for the recipe.*
- *The grapefruit segments should be about the same size as the veal. If they are too large, cut them in half.*
- *Bought grapefruit segments can be used. Make sure they are natural, without added sugar.*
- *Oyster sauce can be bought in the Asian section of most supermarkets.*

countdown

- *Marinate veal.*
- *Boil rice.*
- *Prepare all the stir-fry ingredients.*
- *Stir-fry veal dish.*
- *Finish snow peas and rice.*

quick-fried diced veal

Sugar substitute equivalent to 2 teaspoons sugar

2 tablespoons oyster sauce

2 medium garlic cloves, crushed

$^3/_4$ pound veal escalopes, cut into 1-inch pieces

1 teaspoon cornstarch

2 teaspoons sesame oil

$^1/_2$ medium cucumber, peeled and cut into 1-inch pieces

1 medium grapefruit, cut into segments

2 tablespoons unsweetened grapefruit juice from fresh grapefruit

Salt and freshly ground black pepper

Mix the sugar substitute, oyster sauce, and garlic together. Marinate the veal in the mixture for 10 minutes. Sprinkle cornstarch over veal and toss. The marinade will be absorbed by the veal.

Heat sesame oil in a wok or skillet. Make sure wok is very hot. Add veal and stir-fry for 2 minutes. Remove from wok and add cucumber, grapefruit, and grapefruit juice. Boil to thicken sauce for 1 minute. Return veal to wok and remove from heat. Add salt and pepper to taste. Serve over snow peas and rice.

Makes 2 servings.

Per serving: 483 calories, 46.4 grams protein, 19.3 grams carbohydrate, 22.9 grams fat (11.6 saturated), 150 milligrams cholesterol, 370 milligrams sodium, 1.8 grams fiber

snow peas and rice

½ cup 30-minute quick-cooking
    brown rice

¼ pound snow peas, trimmed

1 teaspoon sesame oil

Salt and freshly ground black
    pepper

Fill a large saucepan with about 2–3 quarts water. Add rice and bring to the boil. Boil for 20 minutes then add the snow peas. Continue to boil for 2–3 minutes. Drain. Toss with sesame oil and salt and pepper to taste. Serve with the veal. *Makes 2 servings.*

Per serving: 132 calories, 4.3 grams protein, 22.3 grams carbohydrate, 3.2 grams fat (0.5 saturated), 0 milligrams cholesterol, 3 milligrams sodium, 2.6 grams fiber

shopping list

FRUIT AND VEG

¼ pound snow peas

1 medium cucumber

1 medium grapefruit

MEAT

³⁄₄ pound veal escalopes

GROCERY

1 small bottle oyster sauce

1 small bottle sesame oil

STAPLES

30-minute quick-cooking
    brown rice

Garlic

Sugar substitute

Cornstarch

Salt

Black peppercorns

five-spice tuna tataki

Tataki—beef or fish that has been seared, thinly sliced, chilled, and served with a dipping sauce—is a tangy, Japanese recipe. Traditional tataki accompaniments are grated daikon (white radish), ginger, chopped scallions, and a dipping sauce.

Japanese and Chinese rice vinegars are made from fermented rice. They're milder than most Western vinegars. White vinegar can be used in this recipe. Add a few drops of water to soften the strength.

Brown rice takes about 45 minutes to cook. There are several brands of quick-cooking brown rice available. Their cooking time ranges from 10 to 30 minutes. I find the 30-minute rice has more flavor, but any quick-cooking rice will work for this dinner.

helpful hints

- Cracked black pepper and five-spice powder can be bought in the spice section of the supermarket.
- Red radishes can be used instead of the daikon or white radish.

countdown

- Sear tuna and let cool slightly.
- Make rice.
- While rice cooks, prepare sauce.
- Make dessert just before serving.

five-spice tuna tataki

2 (6-ounce) tuna steaks
1 tablespoon cracked black pepper
1$^1/_2$ tablespoons sesame oil
2 tablespoons low-sodium soy sauce
2 medium garlic cloves, crushed
$^1/_4$ teaspoon five-spice powder
1 small daikon (white) radish, grated (optional)

Roll tuna steaks in black pepper. Heat $^1/_2$ tablespoon sesame oil in a small nonstick skillet over high heat. Sear tuna for 2 minutes. Turn and sear second side for 2 minutes. Remove to a chopping board and thinly slice.

Mix soy sauce, remaining tablespoon sesame oil, garlic, and five-spice powder together in a small bowl. Serve sliced tuna on 2 individual dinner plates and spoon sauce on top. Sprinkle with grated daikon radish.
Makes 2 servings.

Per serving: 335 calories, 37.3 grams protein, 2.5 grams carbohydrate, 18.0 grams fat (3.4 saturated), 59 milligrams cholesterol, 677 milligrams sodium, 0 grams fiber

japanese brown rice

⅓ cup 30-minute quick-cooking brown rice

¼ pound button mushrooms, sliced

¼ pound fresh snow peas, trimmed

½ cup fat-free, low-sodium chicken broth

1 tablespoon rice vinegar

2 tablespoons low-sodium soy sauce

Salt and freshly ground black pepper

Bring a large saucepan with 2–3 quarts of water to the boil. Add rice and boil for 25 minutes. Add mushrooms and snow peas and continue to boil for 5 minutes. Drain. Mix chicken broth, vinegar, and soy sauce together and toss with rice and vegetables. Add salt and pepper to taste.

Makes 2 servings.

Per serving: 125 calories, 6.1 grams protein, 22.1 grams carbohydrate, 1.1 grams fat (0.1 saturated), 0 milligrams cholesterol, 750 milligrams sodium, 2.4 grams fiber

raspberry banana cooler

1 cup frozen raspberries (not in sugar syrup)

½ medium banana, sliced

1 cup diet lemon-lime

1 cup ice cubes

Sugar substitute equivalent to 2 teaspoons sugar

Place raspberries, banana, diet lemon-lime, ice cubes, and sugar substitute in a blender or food processor and blend until smooth. Serve in tall glasses.

Makes 2 servings.

Per serving: 66 calories, 1.1 grams protein, 16.4 grams carbohydrate, 0.6 grams fat (0.1 saturated), 0 milligrams cholesterol, 1 milligram sodium, 3.5 grams fiber

shopping list

FRUIT AND VEG

1 small daikon (white) radish

1 medium banana

¼ pound button mushrooms

¼ pound fresh snow peas

SEAFOOD

2 (6-ounce) tuna steaks

GROCERY

1 small jar five-spice powder

1 small pack frozen raspberries (not in sugar syrup)

1 small can/bottle diet lemon-lime

1 small bottle rice vinegar

1 small jar cracked black pepper

1 small bottle sesame oil

STAPLES

Garlic

Quick-cooking brown rice

Sugar substitute

Fat-free, low-sodium chicken broth

Low-sodium soy sauce

Salt

Black peppercorns

helpful hints

- Look for roasted chicken that is not marinated in honey or a barbecue sauce. These sauces usually contain sugar.
- This recipe calls for serving the chicken at room temperature. For a hot meal, microwave chicken on high for 2 minutes.

countdown

- Start rice.
- Make salsa.
- Assemble salad.

chicken with black bean salsa and brown rice

Roasted chicken served over rice with a black bean and corn salsa dresses up store-bought roasted or rotisserie chicken breasts.

Sweet vermouth gives this black bean and corn salsa an intriguing flavor. Use the salsa dressing in the recipe or add vermouth and cumin to a bottled low-fat vinaigrette dressing. Brown rice takes about 45 minutes to cook. There are several brands of quick-cooking brown rice available. Their cooking time ranges from 10 to 30 minutes. I find the 30-minute rice has more flavor, but any quick-cooking rice will work for this dinner.

brown rice

$^3/_4$ cup 30-minute quick-cooking brown rice

1 tablespoon plus 1 teaspoon canola oil, divided use

$^1/_2$ tablespoon plus 1 teaspoon sweet (rosso) vermouth

Salt and freshly ground black pepper

First, prepare the brown rice. Bring a large saucepan with 2–3 quarts of water to the boil. Add rice and boil, uncovered, for about 30 minutes (or follow package instructions). Drain into a sieve in the sink. Run hot water through rice and stir with a fork. Return rice to saucepan and add 1 teaspoon canola oil, 1 teaspoon vermouth, and salt and pepper to taste.

chicken with black bean salsa

1 teaspoon ground cumin

Several drops hot pepper sauce

1/4 cup canned black beans, rinsed and drained

1/4 cup frozen corn kernels, defrosted

3/4 pound roasted chicken breast, bones and skin removed

1/4 cup chopped fresh cilantro

2 small tomatoes, cut into wedges

Salt and freshly ground black pepper

While rice cooks, mix 1 tablespoon canola oil, tablespoon vermouth, cumin, hot pepper sauce, and salt and pepper to taste in a medium-sized bowl. Add the black beans and corn. Toss well. Taste and add more seasoning if needed.
Spoon rice on to 2 dinner plates. Slice chicken and place on rice. Spoon salsa on top and sprinkle with cilantro. Arrange tomatoes on the side of the dinner plates.
Makes 2 servings.

Per serving: 558 calories, 32.0 grams protein, 38.4 grams carbohydrate, 18.4 grams fat (3.2 saturated), 144 milligrams cholesterol, 146 milligrams sodium, 2.6 grams fiber

shopping list

FRUIT AND VEG

1 small bunch cilantro

2 small tomatoes

MEAT

3/4 pound roasted chicken breast, bones and skin removed

GROCERY

1 small bottle sweet (rosso) vermouth

1 small can black beans

1 small pack frozen corn kernels

STAPLES

Quick-cooking brown rice

Canola oil

Ground cumin

Hot pepper sauce

Salt

Black peppercorns

veal piccata

Tender veal escalopes are sautéed in a wine and lemon sauce for this quick meal. Garlic zucchinis and tomatoes take only minutes in the microwave oven.

veal piccata

2 tablespoons flour

Salt and freshly ground black
    pepper

³/₄ pound veal escalopes

1 teaspoon olive oil

2 tablespoons fresh lemon juice

2 tablespoons dry vermouth

¼ cup fat-free, low-sodium
    chicken broth

2 tablespoons chopped fresh
    parsley (optional)

Season flour with salt and pepper to taste. Dip veal in flour and shake off excess. Heat oil in a medium-sized nonstick skillet on medium-high heat. When oil is very hot, brown veal on both sides, about 1 minute per side. Sprinkle lemon juice on top. Remove veal to a plate and cover with foil to keep warm. Raise heat to high and add vermouth and chicken broth to the pan. Reduce the liquid by half, takes about 3 minutes. Add salt and pepper to taste. Spoon sauce over veal and sprinkle with parsley.

Makes 2 servings.

Per serving: 424 calories, 44.2 grams protein, 12.4 grams carbohydrate, 19.1 grams fat (10.4 saturated),138 milligrams cholesterol, 177 milligrams sodium, 0.6 grams fiber

helpful hints

- The vegetables can be sautéed instead of cooking them in a microwave oven. Heat the oil in a nonstick skillet, add the vegetables, cover with a lid, and cook for 10 minutes.

countdown

- Boil water for orzo.
- Prepare all ingredients.
- Boil orzo.
- While orzo boils, microwave vegetables.
- Sauté veal.

garlic zucchinis and tomato orzo

1/3 cup orzo (rice-shaped pasta)

1/2 pound zucchinis, cut into 1-inch pieces

1 medium tomato, cut into 1-inch pieces

2 medium garlic cloves, crushed

2 teaspoons olive oil

Salt and freshly ground black pepper

Bring a large saucepan filled with 3–4 quarts water to the boil. Add orzo and boil for 8 minutes. Drain. Meanwhile, place zucchinis, tomatoes and garlic in a microwave-safe bowl. Cover with plastic wrap or a plate and microwave on high for 3 minutes. Remove, stir and microwave on high for 1 minute. Remove and add orzo, olive oil and salt and pepper to taste. Toss well.

Makes 2 servings.

Per serving: 157 calories, 4.5 grams protein, 23.3 grams carbohydrate, 5.1 grams fat (0.7 saturated), 0 milligrams cholesterol, 6 milligrams sodium, 1.2 grams fiber

shopping list

FRUIT AND VEG

  1 small bunch parsley (optional)

  1/2 pound zucchinis

  1 medium tomato

MEAT

  3/4 pound veal escalopes

GROCERY

  1 small bottle dry vermouth

  1 small pack orzo

STAPLES

  Lemons

  Garlic

  Flour

  Olive oil

  Fat-free, low-sodium chicken broth

  Salt

  Black peppercorns

right carbs

Great food that's good for you too is the goal of this third phase, which is designed to become your permanent lifestyle. This is an overall balanced approach to eating. The right-carb phase approximates to a 40-30-30 dietary profile. While there are differences of opinion, it is generally agreed that fat levels (primarily mono-unsaturated) should make up to 30 percent of one's diet. Carbohydrate intake should be restricted to 30 percent more than protein intake. So if the calories from protein are 30 percent of one's diet, the correct carbohydrate level should be 40%. Here in these recipes, high-fiber carbohydrates are incorporated into breakfast, lunch, and dinner menus.

Following the Right Carb 14-Day Meal Plan you will consume an average of 135-145 grams of carbohydrates per day. Carbohydrate percentage is based on carbohydrates less fiber consumed, which is the normal way of calculating carbohydrate consumption. The balance of these meals is 39 percent of calories from carbohydrates, 31 percent of calories from lean protein, 20 percent of calories from mono-unsaturated fat and 6 percent of calories from unsaturated fat.

As with the other sections, I have organized the menus into a meal-at-a-glance chart with some easy and quick meals for mid-week and those that take a little more time for the weekends. They are arranged to give variety throughout the day and over the course of the week. Presentation is as ever important and the appeal of a beautiful plate of food adds to our eating experience. Celebrating events and holidays with friends and cooking for them is a pleasure and almost all the recipes here can be used for special occasions.

Breakfast

Mediterranean Scramble on Toast and Monte Cristo Sandwich are two of the savory breakfasts you can choose from. Try them all to add variety to your morning repertoire. Your body does need a boost of energy in the morning to set you up for the day, both mentally and physically, so don't skimp here.

Lunch

Choose from the wide variety to fit every appetite. When you're in a hurry, grab a BLT Sandwich on Rye or Chicory and Orange Salad with Swiss Turkey. The quality of the ingredients is important with simply prepared food. When you have more time, enjoy the Blue Cheese and Beef Pasta Salad.

Dinner

Enjoy these meals without worrying about numbers or questioning what you eat. The old saying that you should breakfast like a King, lunch like a Prince and dine like a Pauper is one of the best pieces of nutritional advice ever given. Menus like Whisky-Soused Salmon and Turkey Gratinée will entice you to stay on this good-carbohydrate, balanced style of eating. Roasted Pepper and Olive Snapper makes a delicious and rounded meal good enough for a King!

For those days when you are really pressed for time, select Mock Hungarian Goulash or Black Bean Soup with Rice from the Super Speed Suppers section of the book. For weekends when you have more time and want something special, try the Pan-Seared Tuna with Mango Salsa, or Indian-Spiced Chicken from the Weekends section of the book.

right carbs 14-day meal plan at a glance

week 1	breakfast	lunch	dinner
sunday	Ham and Pepper Frittata 95	Mulligatawny Soup 103	Pan-Seared Tuna with Mango Salsa.............158
monday	Smoked Salmon Sandwich...................96	BLT Sandwich on Rye.............................104	Chicken Creole..........136
tuesday	Strawberry Splash with Cottage Cheese-Stuffed Endive 97	Layered Antipasto Salad 105	Mahi Mahi Satay with Thai Peanut Sauce.............112
wednesday	Microwave Portobello Scramble 98	Blue Cheese and Beef Pasta Salad.........................106	Turkey-Gratinée with Basil Linguine...................114
thursday	Mediterranean Scramble on Toast 99	Endive and Orange Salad with Swiss Turkey 107	Parmesan Sole..........135
friday	Monte Cristo Sandwich 100	Mushroom and Sausage Soup..........................108	Roast Pork with Strawberry Salsa.........................111
saturday	Provençal Omelette 101	Danish Shrimp Smorrebrod 109	Indian-Spiced Chicken..................157

week 2	breakfast	lunch	dinner
sunday	Ham and Pepper Frittata 95	Mulligatawny Soup 103	Whisky-Soused Salmon 116
monday	Smoked Salmon Sandwich...................96	BLT Sandwich on Rye............................104	Roasted Pepper and Olive Snapper 118
tuesday	Strawberry Splash with Cottage Cheese-Stuffed Endive 97	Layered Antipasto Salad 105	Hawaiian Chicken with Pineapple Caesar Salad.......................120
wednesday	Microwave Portobello Scramble 98	Blue Cheese and Beef Pasta Salad.......................106	Black Bean Soup with Rice...........................138
thursday	Mediterranean Scramble on Toast 99	Endive and Orange Salad with Swiss Turkey 107	Mock Hungarian Goulash....................139
friday	Monte Cristo Sandwich 100	Mushroom and Sausage Soup...........................108	Mexican Sopes 122
saturday	Provençal Omelette 101	Danish Shrimp Smørrebrød 109	Pork Chops with Apple Relish....................160

right carbs
breakfasts

ham, red pepper, and onion frittata

Plump, juicy frittatas take about 10 minutes to make. They can be made ahead and eaten at room temperature. They differ from omelettes. An omelette is cooked quickly over high heat, making it creamy and runny, while a frittata is cooked slowly over low heat, making it firm and set. A frittata needs to be cooked on both sides. It can be flipped over in the pan, but a much easier way is to place it in the oven or under a broiler for half a minute to finish cooking.

ham, red pepper, and onion frittata

Olive oil spray
1 cup sliced onion
6 ounces sliced lean ham, cut into
    bite-sized pieces
1 medium red bell pepper, sliced
1 cup egg substitute
Salt and freshly ground black
    pepper

Pre-heat broiler. Heat an ovenproof medium-sized nonstick skillet on medium-high heat and spray with olive oil spray. Add onion, ham, and red bell pepper. Cook for 2 minutes. Mix egg substitute with salt and pepper to taste. Reduce heat to low and add egg mixture. Cook, without browning the bottom, for 10 minutes. The eggs will be set, but the top a little runny. Place pan under the broiler for $1/2$–1 minute until the top is set, but not brown. Remove and cut in half. Slide halves on to 2 plates.
Makes 2 servings.

bran cereal

1 cup skim milk
3 ounces high-fiber, no-sugar-
    added bran cereal

Divide ingredients between 2 cereal bowls.
Makes 2 servings.

vegetable juice

$1^{1}/_{2}$ cups low-sodium, no-sugar-
    added tomato or V-8 juice

Divide between 2 glasses.
Makes 2 servings.

Per serving: 366 calories, 38.1 grams protein, 50.6 grams carbohydrate, 7.6 grams fat (2.3 saturated), 42 milligrams cholesterol, 1178 milligrams sodium, 14.5 grams fiber

helpful hints

● *Be careful when removing the skillet from the broiler. The handle will be very hot and remain hot for several minutes after it is removed. Place a pot holder or oven glove over the handle for safety.*

countdown

● *Pre-heat the broiler.*
● *Make frittata.*
● *While frittata cooks, assemble cereal.*

shopping list

FRUIT AND VEG
    1 medium red bell pepper
DELI
    6 ounces sliced lean ham
STAPLES
    Onion
    Egg substitute
    Olive oil spray
    Skim milk
    High-fiber, no-sugar-added
        bran cereal
    Low-sodium, no-sugar-
        added tomato or V-8 juice
    Salt
    Black peppercorns

smoked salmon sandwich

Buttery, smooth smoked salmon is a special breakfast treat.

smoked salmon sandwich

2 slices rye bread
2 tablespoons reduced-fat cream cheese
6 ounces smoked salmon
1 medium tomato, sliced

Toast rye bread and spread with cream cheese. Divide smoked salmon in half and place over cream cheese on each piece of toast. Serve sandwiches with sliced tomato on the side. *Makes 2 servings.*

oatmeal

1 cup oatmeal
2 cups water
1 cup skim milk
Sugar substitute equivalent to 2 teaspoons sugar (optional)

To prepare in the microwave, combine oatmeal and water together. Microwave on high for 4 minutes. Stir in milk and sugar substitute. Alternatively, combine oatmeal and water in a small saucepan. Bring to the boil. Cook for about 5 minutes over medium heat, stirring occasionally. Stir in milk and sugar substitute. *Makes 2 servings.*

Per serving: 416 calories, 28.7 grams protein, 50.7 grams carbohydrate, 11.0 grams fat (4.9 saturated), 39 milligrams cholesterol, 985 milligrams sodium, 5.6 grams fiber

Smoked Salmon Sandwich   **p96**

Strawberry Splash p97

strawberry splash

Sweet strawberries flavor this quick shake that you can make and take on the run.

strawberry splash

1 cup soy milk
2 cups strawberries
1 teaspoon vanilla extract
Sugar substitute equivalent to
   2 teaspoons sugar

Place soy milk, strawberries, vanilla extract, and sugar substitute in a blender and blend until smooth. Divide between 2 glasses.
Makes 2 servings.

cottage cheese-stuffed chicory

1 cup low-fat cottage cheese
2 tablespoons pecan pieces
2 tablespoons snipped dill or
   ½ teaspoon dried
1 small head Belgian endive

Mix cottage cheese, pecans, and dill together. Remove leaves from endive and fill with cottage cheese mixture. Divide between 2 plates.
Makes 2 servings.

bran cereal

1 cup skim milk
1 cup high-fiber, no-sugar-added
   bran cereal

Divide ingredients between 2 cereal bowls.
Makes 2 servings.

Per serving: 387 calories, 24.6 grams protein,
54.8 grams carbohydrate,13.7 grams fat
(2.6 saturated), 12 milligrams cholesterol,
610 milligrams sodium, 16.9 grams fiber

helpful hints

● *Frozen or fresh strawberries can be used. Make sure frozen ones are not packed in sugar syrup.*
● *Use any type of berries.*
● *The stuffed Belgian endive can be made the night before and wrapped in plastic wrap.*
● *The easiest way to chop dill leaves is to snip them right off the stem with scissors.*
● *Dried dill can be used.*

countdown

● *Make shake.*
● *Assemble stuffed Belgian endive.*

shopping list

FRUIT AND VEG
   1 container strawberries
      (10 ounces needed)
   1 small bunch fresh dill (or
      dried dill in a jar)
   1 small head Belgian endive
DAIRY
   1 small carton soy milk
      (8 ounces needed)
   1 cup low-fat cottage cheese
GROCERY
   1 small bottle vanilla extract
   1 small package pecan pieces
STAPLES
   Skim milk
   Sugar substitute
   High-fiber, no-sugar-added
      bran cereal

helpful hints

- Buy thinly sliced portobello or other type of mushrooms.
- Buy good-quality Parmesan cheese and grate it yourself or chop it in the food processor. Freeze extra for quick use. You can quickly spoon out what you need and leave the rest frozen.

countdown

- Assemble cereal.
- Make eggs.

shopping list

FRUIT AND VEG

1 package sliced portobello mushrooms (4 ounces)

STAPLES

Rye bread

Parmesan cheese

Egg substitute

High-fiber, no-sugar-added bran cereal

Olive oil

Grated nutmeg

Skim milk

Salt

Black peppercorns

microwave portobello scramble

The earthy flavor of the portobello mushrooms and the distinctive taste of Parmesan cheese give these microwaved scrambled eggs a rich flavor.

microwave portobello scramble

2 slices rye bread

1/4 pound sliced portobello mushrooms

2 teaspoons olive oil

1 cup egg substitute

3 tablespoons Parmesan cheese

Pinch grated nutmeg

Salt and freshly ground black pepper

Toast rye bread and place on 2 plates. Place mushrooms in a microwave-safe bowl and drizzle with olive oil. Microwave on high for 1 minute. Whisk together egg substitute, Parmesan cheese, nutmeg, and salt and pepper to taste in a bowl. Remove mushrooms from microwave and stir. Pour in egg mixture and stir. Return bowl to microwave oven and microwave on high for 1 1/2 minutes. Remove and stir. Return for another 1 minute. Divide into two portions and spoon on to toast.

Makes 2 servings.

bran cereal

1 cup skim milk

1 cup high-fiber, no-sugar-added bran cereal

Divide ingredients between 2 cereal bowls.

Makes 2 servings.

Per serving: 365 calories, 27.3 grams protein, 49.1 grams carbohydrate, 11.5 grams fat (3.7 saturated), 13 milligrams cholesterol, 894 milligrams sodium, 14.9 grams fiber

mediterranean scramble on toast

Seasoned olives chopped and mixed with spices provide a savory accent for these quick scrambled eggs on toast.

mediterranean scramble on toast

2 slices whole wheat bread

2 tablespoons olive tapenade

Olive oil spray

1 cup egg substitute

2 tablespoons grated Parmesan
   cheese

Freshly ground black pepper

Toast bread and spread with olive tapenade. Heat a small skillet skillet on medium-high heat and spray with olive oil spray. Mix egg substitute with Parmesan cheese and pepper to taste. Pour into pan and cook for 2–3 minutes or until eggs are set. Divide in half and spoon on toast.
Makes 2 servings.

oatmeal

1 cup oatmeal

2 cups water

1 cup skim milk

Sugar substitute equivalent to
   2 teaspoons sugar (optional)

To prepare in the microwave, combine oatmeal and water together. Microwave on high for 4 minutes. Stir in milk and sugar substitute.

Alternatively, combine oatmeal and water in a small saucepan. Bring to the boil. Cook about 5 minutes over medium heat, stirring occasionally. Stir in milk and sugar substitute.
Makes 2 servings.

Per serving: 383 calories, 29.2 grams protein, 46.3 grams carbohydrate, 9.4 grams fat (2.8 saturated), 9 milligrams cholesterol, 700 milligrams sodium, 7 grams fiber

helpful hints

● *Buy good-quality Parmesan cheese and grate it yourself or chop it in the food processor. Freeze extra for quick use. You can quickly spoon out what you need and leave the rest frozen.*

countdown

● *Toast bread and spread with olive tapenade.*
● *Make eggs.*

shopping list

GROCERY
   1 small jar olive tapenade
STAPLES
   Egg substitute
   Parmesan cheese
   Skim milk
   Oatmeal
   Olive oil spray
   Whole wheat bread
   Sugar substitute
   Black peppercorns

monte cristo sandwich

helpful hints

- *Buy turkey breast without added sugar. Honey-coated and barbecued turkey should be avoided as the glazes are sugar based.*

countdown

- *Make sandwich.*
- *Assemble cereal.*

shopping list

DAIRY

1 small package reduced-fat Swiss or Gruyère cheese (2 ounces needed)

DELI

1 small package sliced turkey breast

STAPLES

Egg substitute

Olive oil spray

Whole wheat bread

High-fiber, no-sugar-added bran cereal

Skim milk

Salt

Black peppercorns

Here's a quick version of an old American staple made with cheese and turkey, dipped in batter and fried or baked.

monte cristo sandwich

2 slices reduced-fat Swiss or Gruyère cheese (2 ounces)
2 slices turkey breast (1 ounce)
4 slices whole wheat bread
1 cup egg substitute
Salt and freshly ground black pepper to taste
Olive oil spray

Place 1 slice Swiss cheese and 1 slice turkey on 1 slice of bread. Cover with second slice of bread. Repeat with remaining cheese, turkey and bread. Beat egg substitute with salt and pepper to taste. Dip closed sandwiches into egg mixture. Place a large nonstick skillet over medium heat and spray with olive oil spray.

Remove sandwiches from egg mixture and place in skillet. Brown for 2 minutes and turn. Cover with a lid and cook for 2 minutes more. Remove to 2 plates, cut sandwiches in half, and serve.

Makes 2 servings.

bran cereal

1 cup skim milk
1 cup high-fiber, no-sugar-added bran cereal

Divide ingredients between 2 cereal bowls.

Makes 2 servings.

Per serving: 372 calories, 40.2 grams protein, 52.5 grams carbohydrate, 8.9 grams fat (3.1 saturated), 27 milligrams cholesterol, 707 milligrams sodium, 19 grams fiber

provençal omelette

The flavors of this omelette remind me of sunny Provence where thyme, parsley, peppers, and tomatoes grow abundantly in the rich soil.

provençal omelette

2 slices multigrain bread
Olive oil spray
½ teaspoon dried thyme
1 cup chopped fresh parsley
½ cup low-sodium, no-sugar-
   added tomato sauce
2 whole eggs
4 egg whites
⅛ teaspoon cayenne pepper
Salt and freshly ground black
   pepper

Toast bread, spray with olive oil spray, and set aside. Mix thyme, parsley, and tomato sauce together and set aside. Heat a medium-sized nonstick skillet over medium-high heat. Place eggs in a bowl and stir in cayenne pepper and salt and pepper to taste. Pour the mixture into the skillet. Let the eggs set for about 30 seconds. Tip the pan and lightly move the eggs so that they all set. Cook for 1½ minutes or until eggs are set. Cook a few seconds longer for firmer eggs.

Spoon tomato sauce on half the omelette and fold the omelette in half. Slide out of the pan by tipping the pan and holding a plate vertically against the side of the pan. Turn the pan and plate to invert the omelette on to the plate. Cut in half and serve on 2 plates with the toast. *Makes 2 servings.*

oatmeal

1 cup oatmeal
2 cups water
1 cup skim milk
Sugar substitute equivalent to
   2 teaspoons sugar (optional)

To prepare in the microwave, combine oatmeal and water together. Microwave on high for 4 minutes. Stir in milk and sugar substitute.

Alternatively, combine oatmeal and water in a small saucepan. Bring to the boil. Cook about 5 minutes over medium heat, stirring occasionally. Stir in milk and sugar substitute. *Makes 2 servings.*

Per serving: 380 calories, 28.9 grams protein, 50.1 grams carbohydrate, 11.2 grams fat (2.6 saturated), 215 milligrams cholesterol, 373 milligrams sodium, 7.8 grams fiber

helpful hints

- Dried thyme is called for. If using dried spices, make sure the bottle is less than 6 months old.

countdown

- Make oatmeal.
- Make omelette.

shopping list

FRUIT AND VEG
  1 small bunch parsley
STAPLES
  Eggs (6 needed)
  Multigrain bread
  Olive oil spray
  Low-sodium, no-sugar-
    added tomato sauce
  Oatmeal
  Dried thyme
  Cayenne pepper
  Skim milk
  Sugar substitute
  Salt
  Black peppercorns

right carbs
lunches

mulligatawny soup

Curry powder and ginger give mulligatawny soup a pungent flavor, while chicken and freshly diced crunchy apple provide a contrast in textures.

Authentic curry powder is a blend of freshly ground spices and herbs such as cardamom, chiles, cinnamon, cloves, cilantro, and cumin and is made fresh every day. Commercial curry powder comes in two forms: standard and Madras, the hotter one.

This soup tastes great the second day. If you have time, make double the recipe and reheat when you want to use it.

mulligatawny soup

2 teaspoons canola oil

1 cup sliced onion

1 medium carrot, sliced

1 celery stalk, sliced

1/2 tablespoon curry powder

1 tablespoon flour

1/2-inch piece fresh ginger, chopped or 1 teaspoon ground ginger

1 1/2 cups fat-free, low-sodium chicken broth

1 cup water

1/2 cup light coconut milk

1/2 pound roasted boneless, skinless chicken breast pieces

Salt and freshly ground black pepper

1 medium apple, cored and cubed

2 tablespoons chopped fresh cilantro (optional)

4 lemon wedges

Heat oil on medium-high heat in a large non-stick saucepan. Add onion, carrot, and celery. Sauté for 5 minutes. Add the curry powder, flour, and ginger and sauté for about 30 seconds. Stir in chicken broth, water, and coconut milk and simmer for 5 minutes. Add chicken and continue to simmer for another 5 minutes. Add salt and pepper to taste. Spoon into 2 bowls. Sprinkle with chopped apple and cilantro. Place lemon wedges on side.
Makes 2 servings.

> Per serving: 337 calories, 32.5 grams protein, 28.8 grams carbohydrate, 12.5 grams fat (3.5 saturated), 72 milligrams cholesterol, 547 milligrams sodium, 2.7 grams fiber

dessert

2 medium pears

Slice pears and divide between 2 dessert plates.
Makes 2 servings.

> Per serving: 98 calories, 0.7 grams protein, 25.1 grams carbohydrate, 0.7 grams fat (0 saturated), 0 milligrams cholesterol, 1 milligram sodium, 4.1 grams fiber

helpful hints

● *Curry powder can be found in the spice section of the supermarket. It loses its freshness after 2–3 months.*

● *The soup tastes even better after letting it stand. Leave it for about 5–10 minutes and reheat if you have time.*

countdown

● *Make soup.*

● *Assemble dessert.*

shopping list

FRUIT AND VEG

1 medium apple

1 small bunch fresh cilantro (optional)

1 small piece fresh ginger (or ground ginger)

2 medium pears

MEAT

1/2 pound roasted boneless, skinless chicken breast pieces

GROCERY

1 small jar curry powder

1 can light coconut milk (4 ounces needed)

STAPLES

Carrot

Celery

Lemon

Onion

Canola oil

Flour

Fat-free, low-sodium chicken broth

Salt

Black peppercorns

BLT sandwich on rye

This bacon, arugula, and tomato on rye bread is a modern version of the classic American bacon, lettuce, and tomato sandwich.

BLT sandwich on rye

1/2 pound lean Canadian bacon, cut into 2-inch strips

2 slices rye bread

2 tablespoons reduced-fat mayonnaise

1 tablespoon frozen chopped onion, defrosted

2 cups fresh arugula, torn into bite-sized pieces

1 medium tomato, sliced

Heat a medium-sized nonstick skillet on medium-high heat and add bacon strips. Sauté for 2–3 minutes. Remove to a plate. Meanwhile, toast bread and mix mayonnaise with onion. Spread toast with mayonnaise mixture. Divide arugula into 2 servings and place on toast. Place tomato slices on the arugula. Top with bacon strips. Serve as open-face sandwiches.
Makes 2 servings.

Per serving: 305 calories, 26.6 grams protein, 22.5 grams carbohydrate, 11.9 grams fat (3.2 saturated), 58 milligrams cholesterol, 1321 milligrams sodium, 1.9 grams fiber

dessert

4 cups watermelon cubes

Divide between 2 dessert bowls.
Makes 2 servings.

Per serving: 99 calories, 1.9 grams protein, 22.1 grams carbohydrate, 1.3 grams fat (0.2 saturated), 0 milligrams cholesterol, 6 milligrams sodium, 1.5 grams fiber

helpful hints

- Any type of salad leaves can be used instead of arugula.
- Bacon can be cooked in microwave for 1 minute.
- Frozen onion can be defrosted in the microwave for 2 minutes.
- Fresh-cut watermelon cubes can be found in the fruit and veg section of some supermarkets.

countdown

- Sauté bacon.
- Toast bread.
- Assemble sandwich.

shopping list

FRUIT AND VEG
  1 container fresh watermelon cubes
  1 bunch arugula
  1 medium tomato
DELI
  1/2 pound lean Canadian bacon
STAPLES
  Rye bread
  Reduced-fat mayonnaise
  Frozen chopped onion

layered antipasto salad

Shrimp, Parmesan curls, tomatoes, roasted red bell pepper, arugula, and lettuce form colorful layers for this antipasto salad that is topped with a flavorful Italian dressing.

layered antipasto salad

2 medium tomatoes

2 tablespoons no-sugar-added oil and vinegar dressing

4 cups washed, ready-to-eat Italian-style salad leaves

2 medium green bell peppers, cut into rings

2 cups sweet pimiento, drained and cut into strips

1 cup arugula, torn into large pieces

2 tablespoons Parmesan curls

1/2 pound peeled, deveined, and cooked shrimp

1 cup red onion slices

Quarter 1 tomato and place in food processor with oil and vinegar dressing. Process to make a sauce. Place salad leaves in a salad bowl. Cover with a layer of sliced green bell pepper. Spread the sweet pimiento on top of the green bell pepper and layer the arugula on top. Slice the second tomato and place it over the arugula. Make Parmesan curls by scraping a potato peeler over the cheese. Place shrimp and Parmesan curls over arugula. Sprinkle with onion slices and dressing mixture. *Makes 2 servings.*

Per serving: 387 calories, 33.3 grams protein, 31.8 grams carbohydrate, 13.5 grams fat (3.5 saturated), 181 milligrams cholesterol, 466 milligrams sodium, 0.4 grams fiber

dessert

1 grapefruit

Cut grapefruit in half with a serrated knife and cut around edge and between segments. Place each half on a dessert plate and serve. *Makes 2 servings.*

Per serving: 39 calories, 0.8 grams protein, 9.9 grams carbohydrate, 0.1 gram fat (0 saturated), 0 milligrams cholesterol, 0 milligrams sodium, 1.3 grams fiber

helpful hints

● *Get cooked, peeled shrimp from the fish counter or frozen food section. Make sure they are of good quality.*

● *Look for washed, ready-to-eat salad selections with many different-colored leaves.*

● *Any type of bowl can be used for the salad. A glass one shows off the colored layers.*

● *Make Parmesan strips by peeling thin strips from the cheese with a potato peeler.*

countdown

● *Prepare ingredients.*

● *Make salad.*

shopping list

FRUIT AND VEG

2 medium tomatoes

1 package washed, ready-to-eat Italian-style salad leaves

2 medium green peppers

1 small bunch arugula

1 grapefruit

SEAFOOD

1/2 pound peeled, deveined, and cooked shrimp

GROCERY

1 jar sweet peppers

STAPLES

Parmesan cheese

No-sugar-added oil and vinegar dressing

Red onion

blue cheese and beef pasta salad

Pasta tossed with sweet ripe pears, tangy blue cheese, and juicy roast beef makes this colorful and tasty lunch.

blue cheese and beef pasta salad

³/₄ cup whole wheat penne pasta

1 medium pear, cored and sliced into 1-inch pieces

¹/₄ pound cubed roast beef

1 cup cherry tomatoes

2 tablespoons no-sugar-added oil and vinegar dressing

Salt and freshly ground black pepper

3 tablespoons crumbled blue cheese

Bring a large saucepan filled with water to the boil. Add the pasta and cook for 10 minutes, or according to package instructions. Do not overcook. Drain into a colander in the sink and run under cold water. Place in a bowl and add pear slices, roast beef, and tomatoes. Add dressing and salt and pepper to taste. Toss well. Sprinkle blue cheese on top.

Makes 2 servings.

> Per serving: 393 calories, 25.0 grams protein, 37.0 grams carbohydrate, 17.4 grams fat (5.6 saturated), 57 milligrams cholesterol, 318 milligrams sodium, 5.6 grams fiber

dessert

1 small bunch grapes

Divide the grapes between 2 dessert bowls.

Makes 2 servings.

> Per serving: 58 calories, 0.6 grams protein, 15.8 grams carbohydrate, 0.3 grams fat (0.1 saturated), 0 milligrams cholesterol, 2 milligrams sodium, 0 grams fiber

endive and orange salad with swiss turkey

Belgian endive and orange segments make a colorful and quick salad. To make this ahead, assemble the salad and the Swiss Turkey, but add the dressing and melt the cheese on the sandwiches just before serving.

Belgian endive and orange salad

2 medium heads Belgian endive
2 medium oranges
1 tablespoon pine nuts
2 tablespoons olive oil and vinegar
   dressing

Wipe endive with damp kitchen paper. Cut 1 inch from the base end of the endive. Slice the endive crossways and place in a bowl. Peel oranges and break or cut into segments. Add to bowl. Place pinenuts on a small foil-lined baking tray and toast under broiler. Sprinkle over salad. Drizzle with dressing. Divide between 2 plates.
Makes 2 servings.

Per serving: 165 calories, 1.7 grams protein, 18.3 grams carbohydrate, 8.9 grams fat (2.2 saturated), 0 milligrams cholesterol, 93 milligrams sodium, 3.2 grams fiber

swiss turkey

¼ pound sliced turkey breast
2 slices multigrain bread
1 ounce sliced reduced-fat Swiss
   or Gruyère cheese
1 medium tomato, sliced

Place turkey on bread and place sliced cheese on top. Place on foil-lined baking tray under a broiler for 2 minutes or until cheese melts.

Divide between 2 plates and place tomato slices on the side. Serve with endive salad.
Makes 2 servings.

Per serving: 193 calories, 26 grams protein, 12.8 grams carbohydrate, 5.1 grams fat (1.9 saturated), 48 milligrams cholesterol, 181 milligrams sodium, 3 grams fiber

melon cup

3 cups melon cubes

Divide melon cubes between 2 dessert bowls.
Makes 2 servings.

Per serving: 86 calories, 2.1 grams protein, 20.1 grams carbohydrate, 0.6 grams fat (0 saturated), 0 milligrams cholesterol, 21 milligrams sodium, 0.8 grams fiber

helpful hints

- *Any type of salad leaf can be used instead of the Belgian endive.*
- *Cubed fresh melon can be found in the fruit and veg section of most supermarkets.*

countdown

- *Pre-heat broiler.*
- *Make salad.*
- *Spoon melon into dessert bowls.*
- *Make sandwich.*

shopping list

FRUIT AND VEG
   2 medium heads Belgian
      endive
   1 tomato
   2 medium oranges
   3 cups melon cubes
DAIRY
   1 small package sliced
      reduced-fat Swiss or
      Gruyère cheese (1 ounce)
DELI
   ¼ pound sliced turkey breast
GROCERY
   1 small package pinenuts
   Multigrain bread
STAPLES
   Olive oil and vinegar dressing

mushroom and sausage soup

Mushrooms and sweet sausages make this a warm and hearty lunch. Make extra and use the next day or freeze.

mushroom and sausage soup

2 teaspoons olive oil
2 cups sliced onion
½ pound low-fat turkey sausages,
    cut into 1-inch pieces
1 pound portobello mushrooms,
    sliced
1½ cups fat-free, low-sodium
    chicken broth
¼ teaspoon grated nutmeg
Salt and freshly ground black
    pepper

Heat oil in a large saucepan on medium-high heat. Add onion and sausage. Sauté for 5 minutes. The onions will be transparent, not brown. Add the mushrooms and sauté for 3 minutes. Add the chicken broth and bring to a simmer. Cook for 15 minutes. Add nutmeg and salt and pepper to taste. Taste and add more nutmeg, if needed.
Makes 2 servings.

Per serving: 349 calories, 25.0 grams protein, 20.2 grams carbohydrate, 16.1 grams fat (3.4 saturated), 60 milligrams cholesterol, 1146 milligrams sodium, 2.5 grams fiber

dessert

4 tangerines

Divide between 2 plates and serve.
Makes 2 servings.

Per serving: 74 calories, 1 gram protein, 18.8 grams carbohydrate, 0.4 grams fat (0 saturated), 0 milligrams cholesterol, 2 milligrams sodium, 3.9 grams fiber

danish shrimp smorrebrod

Pretty Danish open sandwiches are attractive and good to eat too.

danish shrimp smorrebrod

1 tablespoon mayonnaise

1 tablespoon freshly squeezed lemon juice

1/2 pound peeled, deveined, and cooked shrimp, sliced

Salt and freshly ground black pepper

2 slices rye bread

2 red-leaf lettuce leaves

1/2 cup diced tomato

Mix mayonnaise and lemon juice together. Add shrimp and salt and pepper to taste. Toss well. Place rye bread on 2 plates. Place a lettuce leaf on each slice. Spoon shrimp on top. Sprinkle diced tomatoes on shrimp.

Makes 2 servings.

Per serving: 263 calories, 26.5 grams protein, 18.8 grams carbohydrate, 8.6 grams fat (1.4 saturated), 176 milligrams cholesterol, 423 milligrams sodium, 1.9 grams fiber

scandinavian cucumber salad

Sugar substitute equivalent to 1 teaspoon sugar

6 tablespoons hot water

2 tablespoons distilled white vinegar

2 tablespoons fresh dill, chopped, or 1 teaspoon dried

1 teaspoon freshly ground black pepper

1 medium cucumber, peeled and thinly sliced

Dissolve the sugar substitute in hot water. When thoroughly dissolved, add vinegar, dill, and black pepper. Mix well. Pour over cucumber and leave to marinate for 10 minutes. Serve with sandwich.

Makes 2 servings.

Per serving: 26 calories, 0.9 grams protein, 6.1 grams carbohydrate, 0.3 grams fat (0 saturated), 0 milligrams cholesterol, 4 milligrams sodium, 0.9 grams fiber

blueberry cup

2 cups blueberries

Divide blueberries between 2 dessert bowls.

Makes 2 servings.

Per serving: 82 calories, 1 gram protein, 20 grams carbohydrate, 0.5 grams fat (0 saturated), 0 milligrams cholesterol, 9 milligrams sodium, 4.4 grams fiber

helpful hints

● *The quickest way to chop fresh dill is to snip the leaves from the stem with scissors.*

● *Any type of leaf lettuce can be used.*

● *Slice cucumber in a food processor fitted with a thin slicing blade. Or thinly slice with a mandoline.*

countdown

● *Make cucumber salad and leave to marinate while preparing sandwich.*

● *Make sandwich.*

shopping list

FRUIT AND VEG

1 medium cucumber

1 medium tomato

1 small head red-leaf lettuce

1 small bunch fresh dill (or dried dill)

1 small punnet blueberries

SEAFOOD

1/2 pound peeled, deveined, and cooked shrimp

STAPLES

Lemon

Rye bread

Mayonnaise

Sugar substitute

Distilled white vinegar

Salt

Black peppercorns

right carbs
dinners

roast pork with strawberry salsa

Pork tenderloin with chunky strawberry salsa makes a sweet and spicy dinner. Strawberries, normally used for dessert, can also be added to salads or used to make tasty condiments for cooked meats.

roast pork with strawberry salsa

3/4 pound pork tenderloin

Olive oil spray

1 1/2 teaspoons ground cumin

2 cups ripe strawberries, hulled and cut into 1/4-inch pieces

Sugar substitute equivalent to 1 teaspoon sugar

1/4 cup diced red onion

Several drops hot pepper sauce

1 tablespoon fresh lime juice

Salt

4 tablespoons chopped fresh cilantro (optional)

Pre-heat broiler. Line a baking tray with foil and place under broiler. Trim fat from pork and cut filet in half lengthways. Spray all sides with olive oil spray. Sprinkle with 1 teaspoon ground cumin. Remove baking tray from broiler and place pork on tray. Broil for 5 minutes. Turn and cook for another 5 minutes. Test pork. A meat thermometer should read 160 degrees.

While pork boils, place strawberries in a medium-sized bowl and sprinkle with sweetener. Add onion and hot pepper sauce. Mix the remaining 1/2 teaspoon cumin and lime juice together and drizzle over berries. Add salt to taste. Toss well and sprinkle with cilantro. Serve pork with salsa on top.
Makes 2 servings.

Per serving: 333 calories, 46.7 grams protein, 13.8 grams carbohydrate, 10.1 grams fat (3.3 saturated), 146 milligrams cholesterol, 115 milligrams sodium, 2.8 grams fiber

zucchini and linguine

4 ounces spinach linguine

1/2 pound zucchini, halved lengthways and sliced

1/2 pound diced red onion

1 tablespoon olive oil

Salt and freshly ground black pepper

Place a large saucepan filled with 3–4 quarts of water on to boil. Add the pasta and boil for 5 minutes. Add the zucchinis and onion and continue to boil for 3 minutes, or until the pasta is cooked through but firm. Drain the pasta and vegetables leaving a few tablespoons of cooking water with the pasta. Toss with the olive oil. Add salt and pepper to taste.
Makes 2 servings.

Per serving: 316 calories, 9.4 grams protein, 52.3 grams carbohydrate, 7.9 grams fat (1.1 saturated), 0 milligrams cholesterol, 6 milligrams sodium, 3.5 grams fiber

helpful hints

- *If you like your salsa hot, add more pepper sauce.*
- *Use any type of berry.*
- *Placing the pork on a pre-heated baking tray helps it to cook faster.*
- *Red onion is used in both recipes. Dice at one time and divide accordingly.*
- *If you come across them, use yellow zucchinis instead of green, to add a contrasting color to the dish.*

countdown

- *Pre-heat broiler and baking tray.*
- *Boil water for pasta.*
- *Broil pork.*
- *Make salsa.*
- *Boil pasta and zucchinis.*

shopping list

FRUIT AND VEG

1 (10-ounce) package ripe strawberries 1 lime

1 small bunch fresh cilantro

1/2 pound zucchini

MEAT

3/4 pound pork tenderloin

GROCERY

4 ounces spinach linguine

STAPLES

Olive oil

Ground cumin

Sugar substitute

Red onions

Hot pepper sauce

Salt

Black peppercorns

mahi mahi satay with thai peanut sauce

Fresh fish, quickly cooked and served with a spicy, peanut sauce, brings back memories of the enticing aroma of satay (Asian kebabs) cooking on small broilers in the street markets of South-east Asia. I've used peanut butter as a base for the spicy peanut sauce to shorten the preparation time.

If using wooden skewers, be sure to soak them in water for about 30 minutes before use. This keeps them from burning under the broiler.

The fish only takes 4 minutes to cook.

Brown rice takes about 45 minutes to cook. There are several brands of quick-cooking brown rice available. Their cooking time ranges from 10 to 30 minutes. I find the 30-minute rice has more flavor, but any quick-cooking rice will work for this dinner.

mahi mahi satay with thai peanut sauce

1 teaspoon canola oil
1 1/2 tablespoon rice vinegar
1 1/2 garlic cloves, bruised
Salt and freshly ground black pepper
3/4 pound mahi mahi
2 x 8-inch wooden or metal skewers
2 tablespoons crunchy peanut butter
1 tablespoon low-sodium soy sauce
Sugar substitute equivalent to 2 teaspoons sugar
6 drops hot pepper sauce

Pre-heat broiler. Mix oil, 1 tablespoon rice vinegar and garlic together. Add salt and pepper to taste. Slice fish into strips about 1/2-inch thick and 4 inches long. Place in the marinade and set aside for 10 minutes, turning after 5 minutes to make sure all sides are marinated. Remove from marinade and thread the fish strips on to the skewers. I find that threading in a wave pattern allows more even cooking. Place on a foil-lined baking tray and broiler for 2 minutes on each side.

To make the peanut sauce: In a small bowl, mix peanut butter, soy sauce and remaining 1/2 tablespoon rice vinegar together until blended to a smooth consistency. Add sugar substitute and hot pepper sauce.

Serve the skewers on a plate with a little of the sauce poured over the fish and the rest on the side for dipping.
Makes 2 servings.

Per serving: 259 calories, 33.8 grams protein, 4.6 grams carbohydrate, 11.6 grams fat (2.1 saturated), 116 milligrams cholesterol, 446 milligrams sodium, 0 grams fiber

snow peas and rice

⅓ cup 30-minute quick-cooking
   brown rice

¼ pound snow peas, trimmed

2 teaspoons canola oil

Salt and freshly ground black
   pepper

Bring a large saucepan filled with 2–3 quarts of water to the boil. Add the rice, stir once or twice, and let boil for 25 minutes. Add the snow peas and continue to boil for 2 minutes. Test a grain; rice should be cooked through, but not soft. Drain into a sieve in the sink and return to the pan. Mix in oil and salt and pepper to taste. *Makes 2 servings.*

Per serving: 153 calories, 4.3 grams protein, 22.3 grams carbohydrate, 5.5 grams fat (0.8 saturated), 0 milligrams cholesterol, 3 milligrams sodium, 2.6 grams fiber

lychee cup

2 cups canned, drained lychees

Divide between 2 dessert bowls. *Makes 2 servings.*

Per serving: 126 calories, 2 grams protein, 32 grams carbohydrate, 0.5 grams fat (0 saturated), 0 milligrams cholesterol, 2 milligrams sodium, 4 grams fiber

shopping list

FRUIT AND VEG
   ¼ pound snow peas

SEAFOOD
   ¾ pound mahi mahi

GROCERY
   1 small bottle rice vinegar
   1 small jar crunchy peanut
      butter
   1 small package 8-inch
      wooden or metal skewers
   1 can lychees

STAPLES
   Canola oil
   Garlic
   30-minute quick-cooking
      brown rice
   Low-sodium soy sauce
   Sugar substitute
   Hot pepper sauce
   Salt
   Black peppercorns

turkey gratinée with basil linguine

A golden, cheesy crust tops this quick turkey and mushroom sauté. The broiled, grated cheese and breadcrumb crust is called a gratin. This meal takes about 10 minutes to complete. Or you can make it ahead and then place it under the broiler just before you need it.

The turkey breast escalopes called for in the recipe are cut about 1/4 inch thick. They only need to be cooked for 1 minute on each side. Watch them carefully. They become dry and tough if overdone.

helpful hints

- Buy good-quality Parmesan cheese and grate it yourself or chop it in the food processor. Freeze extra for quick use. You can quickly spoon out what you need and leave the rest frozen.
- Chicken escalopes can be substituted for turkey.
- Any green herb can be substituted for the basil.
- Fresh pineapple cubes can be found in the fruit and veg section of many supermarkets.

countdown

- Pre-heat broiler.
- Make dessert.
- Boil water for pasta.
- Make turkey.
- Make pasta.

turkey gratinée

1 teaspoon olive oil

1/2 pound turkey breast escalopes (about 1/4 inch thick)

Salt and freshly ground black pepper

1 cup frozen chopped onion

2 medium garlic cloves, crushed

1/2 pound portobello mushrooms, sliced

1 tablespoon flour

1/2 cup skim milk

1/4 cup plain breadcrumbs

2 tablespoons grated Parmesan cheese

Pre-heat broiler. Heat oil in a medium-sized nonstick ovenproof skillet over medium-high heat. Brown turkey for 1 minute, then turn and brown second side for 1 minute. Remove to a plate and sprinkle with salt and pepper to taste.

Add onion, garlic, and mushrooms to pan and sauté for 2 minutes. Add flour and continue to sauté for 30 seconds. Add milk and stir for 2 minutes to thicken sauce. Push mushrooms to sides of skillet and return turkey to the pan.

Cover turkey with mushrooms and sprinkle with breadcrumbs and Parmesan cheese. Add salt and pepper to taste. Place under broiler for 2 minutes.

Makes 2 servings.

Per serving: 355 calories, 41.3 grams protein, 18.7 grams carbohydrate, 10.2 grams fat (3.5 saturated), 88 milligrams cholesterol, 312 milligrams sodium, 0 grams fiber

basil linguine

1/4 pound fresh linguine
2 teaspoons olive oil
1/2 cup chopped fresh basil
Salt and freshly ground black
    pepper

Bring a large saucepan filled with 3–4 quarts of water to the boil. When water comes to the boil, add pasta and cook 3 minutes for fresh pasta or 9 minutes for dried. Drain, leaving about 2 tablespoons pasta water with the pasta. Add olive oil to pasta and toss well. Add basil and salt and pepper to taste.

Makes 2 servings.

Per serving: 219 calories, 5.8 grams protein, 35.7 grams carbohydrate, 5.4 grams fat (0.7 saturated), 0 milligrams cholesterol, 1 milligram sodium, 2.1 grams fiber

spiced pineapple

1/2 teaspoon ground allspice
Sugar substitute equivalent to
    2 teaspoons sugar
2 cups pineapple cubes

Mix allspice and sugar substitute together. Place pineapple cubes in a microwave-safe bowl. Sprinkle spice mixture on top and toss to make sure all cubes are coated with the mixture. Place in microwave oven and microwave on high for 1 minute. Remove and divide between 2 dessert bowls.

Makes 2 servings.

Per serving: 77 calories, 0.6 grams protein, 20.2 grams carbohydrate, 0.7 grams fat (0 saturated), 0 milligrams cholesterol, 1 milligrams sodium, 2.4 grams fiber

shopping list

FRUIT AND VEG
   1 small bunch fresh basil
   1/2 pound sliced portobello
      mushrooms
   1 container pineapple cubes
MEAT
   1/2 pound turkey breast
      escalopes (about 1/4-inch
      thick)
GROCERY
   1 small jar ground allspice
   1/4 pound fresh linguine
   1 small package plain
      breadcrumbs
STAPLES
   Olive oil
   Garlic
   Frozen chopped onions
   Skim milk
   Flour
   Parmesan cheese
   Sugar substitute
   Salt
   Black peppercorns

whisky-soused salmon

Salmon, potatoes, and whisky combine to star in this quick dinner. Salmon can be bought as thick steaks with the bone in or as thin fillets.

helpful hints

- The quickest way to wash watercress is to place it leaves first into a bowl of water. Leave for a minute, then lift out and shake dry.
- A quick way to chop chives is to cut them with scissors.

countdown

- Make dessert
- Boil potatoes.
- Make salmon sauce.
- Poach salmon.
- Add broccoli and finish potatoes.

whisky-soused salmon

2 x (6-ounce) salmon steaks
2 cups water
Pinch salt
1/4 cup reduced-fat mayonnaise
1 tablespoon fresh lemon juice
1 tablespoon whisky
Several sprigs of watercress

Rinse salmon. Bring water to the boil and add salt. Place salmon in water. Liquid should completely cover salmon. Add more water, if needed. Bring to a simmer and gently cook for 5 minutes. Salmon will be opaque. Remove to individual plates.

Whisk mayonnaise, lemon juice, and whisky together in a small bowl and spoon over salmon. Place several sprigs of watercress on the side. Makes 2 servings.

Per serving: 286 calories, 38.6 grams protein, 0.8 grams carbohydrate, 9.8 grams fat (2.3 saturated), 111 milligrams cholesterol, 114 milligrams sodium, 0 grams fiber

broccoli and potatoes

1/2 pound new potatoes, washed and cut into 11/2-inch pieces

2 cups broccoli florets

2 teaspoons olive oil

Salt and freshly ground black pepper

2 tablespoons snipped chives

Place potatoes in a large saucepan and cover with cold water. Cover with a lid and bring to the boil. Lower heat to medium and simmer for 5 minutes. Add the broccoli florets and continue to cook, covered, for 5 minutes. Drain, remove to a bowl, and toss with olive oil and salt and pepper to taste. Sprinkle with chives. Toss well. *Makes 2 servings.*

Per serving: 159 calories, 5.1 grams protein, 25.2 grams carbohydrate, 5.1 grams fat (0.6 saturated), 0 milligrams cholesterol, 27 milligrams sodium, 3.0 grams fiber

deep dish blueberry cream

1 tablespoon cornstarch

Sugar substitute equivalent to 2 teaspoons sugar

2 cups blueberries

1 cup water

1 cup nonfat vanilla yogurt

In a small cup, mix cornstarch and sugar. Stir this mixture into water placed in a medium-sized saucepan. Bring to the boil over high heat and allow to thicken. Add 1/3 cup blueberries and boil for 3 minutes. Remove from heat. Divide yogurt between 2 ramekins. Spoon the remaining berries on top. Spoon sauce over berries. Refrigerate until needed. *Makes 2 servings.*

Per serving: 192 calories, 6.5 grams protein, 41.6 grams carbohydrate, 0.6 grams fat (0 saturated), 3 milligrams cholesterol, 104 milligrams sodium, 4.4 grams fiber

shopping list

FRUIT AND VEG

1/2 pound new potatoes

1 small package broccoli florets

1 small bunch fresh chives

1 small bunch watercress

1 small punnet blueberries

DAIRY

1 pot nonfat vanilla yogurt

SEAFOOD

2 x (6-ounce) salmon steaks

GROCERY

1 small bottle whisky

STAPLES

Olive oil

Reduced-fat mayonnaise

Lemon

Cornstarch

Sugar substitute

Salt

Black peppercorns

helpful hints

- Any type of olive can be used.
- Any type of fish fillet can be used. Allow 10 minutes cooking time for each inch of thickness.

countdown

- Make eggs.
- Arrange salad on 2 plates.

roasted pepper and olive snapper

Fresh snapper, roasted red peppers, and Greek olives are broiled for only 8 minutes for this simple Greek meal. This quick meal was inspired by a trip to Greece. We drove to Delphi along a road bordered by an endless sea of olive trees. These amazing groves contained over a million trees. The view over this olive carpet leading to the blue sea was spectacular.

Brown rice takes about 45 minutes to cook. There are several brands of quick-cooking brown rice available. Their cooking time ranges from 10 to 30 minutes. I find the 30-minute rice has more flavor, but any quick-cooking rice will work for this dinner.

roasted pepper and olive snapper

2 x (6-ounce) snapper fillets
1 tablespoon olive oil
Salt and freshly ground black pepper
1½ cups sliced sweet pimiento, drained
8 pitted black olives, cut in half

Pre-heat broiler. Wash fish fillets and pat dry with kitchen paper. Place in a small, shallow ovenproof dish. Drizzle olive oil on top. Sprinkle with salt and pepper to taste.

Place pimiento slices and olives around fish. Broil for 8 minutes. If fillet is 1-inch thick, broil for 10 minutes. Serve fish on 2 plates and spoon roasted peppers and olives on top.
Makes 2 servings.

Per serving: 296 calories, 33.6 grams protein, 15.2 grams carbohydrate, 11.5 grams fat (1.5 saturated), 57 milligrams cholesterol, 694 milligrams sodium, 3 grams fiber

lemon-braised celery hearts and rice

1 cup fat-free, low-sodium chicken
    broth

1 cup water

6 medium celery stalks, tender
    lower sections only, cut into
    2-inch pieces

1/3 cup 30-minute quick-cooking
    brown rice

1 tablespoon freshly squeezed
    lemon juice

2 teaspoons olive oil

1/4 cup raisins

Salt and freshly ground black
    pepper

Pour chicken broth and water into a saucepan and bring to the boil on high heat. Add celery and rice, and reduce heat to medium. Cover with a lid and simmer for 30 minutes until stalks are tender but still firm.

Drain, reserving 3 tablespoons liquid. Remove to a shallow bowl. Mix lemon juice, olive oil, and cooking liquid together and add raisins, salt, and pepper to taste. Pour over rice and celery.
Makes 2 servings.

Per serving: 184 calories, 3.4 grams protein, 33.1 grams carbohydrate, 5.5 grams fat (0.8 saturated), 0 milligrams cholesterol, 54 milligrams sodium, 1 gram fiber

peach crumble

3 medium peaches, stones
    removed and sliced

2 tablespoons flour

Sugar substitute equivalent to
    2 teaspoons sugar

1 tablespoon butter

Place peach slices in an oven-to-table bowl that can also be used in a microwave oven. Microwave fruit on high for 2 minutes. Mix flour and sweetener together. Cut in butter, and rub with fingertips to make a crumbly mixture. Spoon over fruit and place under broiler for 5 minutes, or until topping is golden.
Makes 2 servings.

Per serving: 138 calories, 1.8 grams protein, 21.6 grams carbohydrate, 5.7 grams fat (3.5 saturated), 16 milligrams cholesterol, 58 milligrams sodium, 0.8 grams fiber

shopping list

FRUIT AND VEG
    1 bunch celery hearts
    3 medium peaches
SEAFOOD
    2 x (6-ounce) snapper fillets
GROCERY
    1 jar sweet peppers
    1 container stoned black
        olives (8 olives needed)
    1 small package raisins
STAPLES
    Olive oil
    Butter
    Flour
    30-minute quick-cooking
        brown rice
    Fat-free, low-sodium chicken
        broth
    Sugar substitute
    Lemon
    Salt
    Black peppercorns

hawaiian chicken with pineapple caesar salad

helpful hints

● *Fresh pineapple cubes can be found in the fruit and veg section of many supermarkets.*

● *Look for no-sugar-added pineapple juice.*

● *I have cooked this chicken in a skillet, because it's faster and easier than heating the broiler for a mid-week dinner. If you have the time, broil the chicken for about 2 minutes per side then move it to a cooler area of the broiler. Add a spoonful of sauce to each piece and cook for 2 more minutes.*

● *To cube a mango, slice off each side as close to the stone as possible. Take the mango half in your hand, skin side down. Score the fruit in a criss-cross pattern through to the skin. Bend the skin backwards so that the cubes pop up. Slice the cubes away from the skin. Repeat with the other half. Score and slice any fruit left on the stone.*

countdown

● *Make dessert and set aside.*

● *Make chicken sauce.*

● *Cook chicken.*

● *Make salad.*

On a trip to Hawaii I met a famous local chef who served me a Hawaiian chicken dish with a pineapple barbecue glaze. I've adapted his ideas for these recipes. Barbecue sauces can be filled with sugar. Here's one you can make with a sweet flavor and not many carbs.

Brown rice takes about 45 minutes to cook. There are several brands of quick-cooking brown rice available. Their cooking time ranges from 10 to 30 minutes. I find the 30-minute rice has more flavor, but any quick-cooking rice will work for this dinner.

hawaiian chicken

2 x (6-ounce) boneless, skinless
  chicken breasts
Olive oil spray
Salt and freshly ground black
  pepper
1/4 cup no-sugar-added pasta
  sauce
2 tablespoons pineapple juice
2 teaspoons Dijon mustard
Sugar substitute equivalent to
  2 teaspoons sugar
1/2 cup 30-minute quick-cooking
  brown rice
1 teaspoon canola oil

Place chicken between 2 layers of greaseproof paper and flatten with a kitchen mallet or the bottom of a heavy pan. Heat a medium-sized nonstick skillet on medium-high heat and spray with olive oil spray. Brown chicken for 2 minutes. Turn and brown for another 2 minutes.

Season both sides with salt and pepper. Lower heat to medium and spoon 1 tablespoon sauce over each piece. Cover with a lid and cook for 2 minutes. A meat thermometer should read 170 degrees. Remove to 2 dinner plates and serve remaining sauce on the side.
Makes 2 servings.

Per serving: 379 calories, 52.4 grams protein, 19.8 grams carbohydrate, 10.5 grams fat (2.1 saturated), 132 milligrams cholesterol, 336 milligrams sodium, 1.3 grams fiber

pineapple caesar salad

2 cups pineapple cubes

4 cups romaine lettuce, torn into
   bite-sized pieces

1/4 cup snipped chives

2 tablespoons no-sugar-added
   Caesar dressing

2 tablespoons grated Parmesan
   cheese

Place pineapple cubes and lettuce in a salad bowl. Add chives and dressing. Toss well. Sprinkle the top with Parmesan cheese. *Makes 2 servings.*

Per serving: 162 calories, 1.5 grams protein, 20.6 grams carbohydrate, 9.7 grams fat (1.5 saturated), 18 milligrams cholesterol, 124 milligrams sodium, 2.6 grams fiber

dessert

2 medium mangoes cut into cubes

Divide mangoes between 2 dessert bowls. *Makes 2 servings.*

Per serving: 134 calories, 1.1 grams protein, 35.2 grams carbohydrate, 0.6 grams fat (0.1 saturated), 0 milligrams cholesterol, 4 milligrams sodium, 2.2 grams fiber

shopping list

FRUIT AND VEG

   1 container fresh pineapple
      cubes (10 ounces needed)

   1 small head romaine lettuce

   1 small bunch chives

   2 medium mangoes

MEAT

   2 x (6-ounce) boneless,
      skinless chicken breasts

GROCERY

   1 small jar/can pineapple
      juice

   1 bottle no-sugar-added
      Caesar dressing

STAPLES

   Parmesan cheese

   Olive oil spray

   Canola oil

   No-sugar-added pasta sauce

   Dijon mustard

   30-minute quick-cooking
      brown rice

   Sugar substitute

   Salt

   Black peppercorns

mexican sopes

On a trip to Mexico City, I watched a local chef make these melt-in-your-mouth sopes. They're little corn tortillas filled with a spicy black bean spread, roasted chicken, lettuce, and cheese. Although sopes are usually served as appetizers, she mentioned that they make quick and easy supper dishes too.

mexican sopes

2 teaspoons canola oil

1/2 cup diced red onion

1/2 cup rinsed and drained canned black beans

Several drops hot pepper sauce

Salt and freshly ground black pepper

1/2 pound roasted or rotisserie chicken breast, skin and bones removed

4 x (6-inch) corn tortillas

1 cup washed, ready-to-eat, shredded lettuce

1/4 cup grated reduced-fat Cheddar cheese

1 cup medium-heat no-sugar-added tomato salsa

Heat 1 teaspoon oil in a large nonstick skillet on medium-high heat. Add half the diced onion and sauté until it starts to shrivel, about 3 minutes. Remove to the bowl of a food processor. Add beans, remaining 1 teaspoon oil and hot pepper sauce, and purée. If you do not have a food processor, mash the beans with a fork and mix with the onion, oil, and hot pepper sauce. If the beans are dry, add a few tablespoons of water. Add salt and pepper to taste. Set aside. Shred chicken into bite-sized pieces.

Place the same skillet over medium-low heat. Add the tortillas and warm for 30 seconds. Turn them over and spread the top of each tortilla with the black bean mixture. Sprinkle with the remaining onion. Layer lettuce, cheese, and chicken over each one. If tortillas do not all fit in pan, cook them 2 at a time. Cover with a lid for 1 minute. Remove to 2 dinner plates. Spoon salsa on top or serve on the side.

Makes 2 servings.

Per serving: 517 calories, 54.8 grams protein, 49.8 grams carbohydrate, 15.6 grams fat (4.1 saturated), 104 milligrams cholesterol, 1112 milligrams sodium, 8.0 grams fiber

oranges in cherry coulis

2 oranges
1 cup frozen sweet, dark cherries

Peel oranges and slice over a bowl to catch the juice. Defrost cherries for 1 minute in a microwave oven. Purée cherries in a food processor, adding juice from peeled oranges, or press cherries through a food mill. Spoon cherry coulis on to 2 dessert plates. Place orange slices on top.

Makes 2 servings.

Per serving: 228 calories, 31.5 grams protein, 4.7 grams carbohydrate, 9.3 grams fat (2.5 saturated), 253 milligrams cholesterol, 215 milligrams sodium, 0 grams fiber

shopping list

FRUIT AND VEG
    1 bag washed, ready-to-eat
        shredded lettuce
    2 oranges
DAIRY
    1 package grated reduced-fat
        Cheddar cheese
MEAT
    1/2 pound roasted or
        rotisserie chicken breast
GROCERY
    1 bag frozen sweet, dark
        cherries
    4 x (6-inch) corn tortillas
STAPLES
    Canola oil
    Red onion
    Canned black beans
    Hot pepper sauce
    Medium-heat, no-sugar-
        added tomato salsa
    Salt
    Black peppercorns

super speed suppers

These meals are for those nights when I haven't got the time to think about dinner, but don't want to send out for something that won't fit my good-carb lifestyle. At the end of the day, when I've just come in and the family needs to be fed, I need a repertoire of super speed suppers that can just be thrown together. It's a good idea to keep a stock of items that are the base of many super speed dishes—like fresh lettuce, from romaine to radicchio and arugula to add varied color and flavor. I've based the recipes in this section on ingredients that I bought from the supermarket that can be assembled into a meal in 15 minutes or less.

Savory Sage Chicken is one of my real favorites and I have made it time and again over the years since first moving to a good-carb lifestyle. It's based on roasted or rotisserie chicken that is doctored at home and you'd be surprised just how much zing it has from the addition of a little dry vermouth. It fits the Quick Start nutritional guidelines and takes about 10 minutes to make from start to finish. Delicious!

I love a good, hearty bowl of soup for supper, even in the summer. The Peasant Country Soup is perfect for a quick dinner. It takes only 10 minutes to make and fits the Which Carb nutritional guidelines. Full of robust flavors, it is deeply satisfying.

When I brought the Mock Hungarian Goulash to the radio station studio for one of my programs, all the staff lined up for seconds. It is made in 10 minutes, uses lean roast beef from the deli, and fits the Right Carbs nutritional guidelines.

Simply prepared food can be just as satisfying as something that's taken hours to make. Shopping is important and choosing the best ingredients you can afford will enhance the pleasure of eating good fresh dishes.

Look for ingredients which have not been covered in sauces and seasonings to cover up for poor quality. Look for vegetables and fruits in season— one of the Super Speed Lunch menus includes melon for dessert and, if you look at the array of different melons in the supermarket, you will see that it is easy to choose a new variety for each day of the week.

These meals have been incorporated into the 2-week menu plan for the appropriate phase. Keep a good store of bottled ingredients on hand and you can throw a dinner together faster than getting into your car or phoning for a take-out. Jerk seasoning, tomato salsa, teriyaki sauce, and Worcestershire sauce are just some of those to have around all the time; there is no end of good-carb ideas that can be made speedily using them.

When I give cooking classes and show these ideas, the response is always surprising—that you can get such flavorful food in such a short time. I've served these meals at dinner parties, too, without telling anyone they were good-carb.

quick start
super speed
suppers

greek shrimp with feta cheese

This meal fits the nutritional guidelines for the Quick Start phase. Greek feta cheese gives this shrimp dish a tangy Mediterranean flavor.

greek shrimp with feta cheese

2 teaspoons olive oil

1/2 cup frozen chopped onion

2 garlic cloves, crushed

1 large tomato, diced

3/4 pound large shrimp, shelled and deveined

1/2 cup crumbled feta cheese

1 teaspoon dried oregano

Salt and freshly ground black pepper

Heat olive oil in a medium-sized nonstick skillet on medium-high heat and add the onion, garlic, and tomato. Sauté for 3 minutes. Add shrimp and sprinkle cheese and oregano on top. Sauté for 3 minutes, turning shrimp to make sure they are cooked on both sides. Remove from heat, cover with a lid, and let sit for 2 minutes, or until cheese melts. Add salt and pepper to taste. *Makes 2 servings.*

Per serving: 349 calories, 41.6 grams protein, 9.6 grams carbohydrate, 14.9 grams fat (6.2 saturated), 280 milligrams cholesterol, 638 milligrams sodium, 0.9 grams fiber

romaine and fresh cabbage salad

2 cups shredded, washed, ready-to-eat cabbage

2 cups shredded, washed, ready-to-eat romaine lettuce

2 scallions, sliced

1 teaspoon dried dill

2 tablespoons olive oil and vinegar dressing

Combine cabbage, lettuce, scallions, and dill in a bowl. Add dressing and toss well. *Makes 2 servings.*

Per serving: 104 calories, 1.4 grams protein, 6.1 grams carbohydrate, 8.7 grams fat (1.3 saturated), 0 milligrams cholesterol, 91 milligrams sodium, 1.2 grams fiber

helpful hints

- *Shredded cabbage can be bought ready-to-eat in the fruit and veg section of some supermarkets.*
- *Crumbled feta cheese can be found in the dairy section of the supermarket.*
- *Dried oregano and dill are used in this recipe. Replace dried herbs after 6 months. If they look grey and old, that's probably how they will taste.*

countdown

- *Assemble salad.*
- *Make shrimp.*

shopping list

FRUIT AND VEG

1 bag shredded, washed, ready-to-eat cabbage

1 bag shredded, washed, ready-to-eat romaine lettuce

1 small bunch scallions

1 large tomato

DAIRY

1 small package crumbled feta cheese

SEAFOOD

3/4 pound large shrimp

STAPLES

Olive oil and vinegar dressing

Olive oil

Frozen chopped onion

Garlic

Dried dill

Dried oregano

Salt

Black peppercorns

jamaican jerk pork

This meal fits the nutritional guidelines for the Quick Start phase.

"Jerking" is an ancient Jamaican method for preserving and cooking meat. In Jamaica the men who prepare the meat and sell it to the markets are called "jerk men." They use a long process involving marinating the meat and then slowly cooking it over a pimiento (allspice) wood fire. I've captured the flavors of jerk cooking for this quick dinner by using a prepared jerk seasoning.

jamaican jerk pork

2 x (6-ounce) boneless pork
  chops, about 1/2-inch thick
1 tablespoon jerk seasoning
1 teaspoon canola oil

Remove fat from pork and rub with jerk seasoning. Heat oil in a medium-sized nonstick skillet on medium-high heat. Add pork and brown for 2 minutes. Turn and brown second side for 2 minutes. Lower heat to medium and cook 2 more minutes. A meat thermometer should read 160 degrees. Makes 2 servings. *Makes 2 servings.*

> Per serving: 287 calories, 45.3 grams protein,
> 1.5 grams carbohydrate, 9.8 grams fat (3.0 saturated),
> 146 milligrams cholesterol, 107 milligrams sodium,
> 0 grams fiber

palm heart salad

1 (14-ounce) can hearts of palm
4 cups washed, ready-to-eat salad
1/2 medium cucumber, peeled and
  sliced
2 tablespoons no-sugar-added oil
  and vinegar dressing
2 medium tomatoes, quartered

Drain hearts of palm and cut into 1-inch slices. Place prepared salad in a bowl and add cucumber and dressing. Toss well. Add tomato wedges along edge of bowl and sprinkle hearts of palm on top.
Makes 2 servings.

> Per serving: 160 calories, 6.8 grams protein,
> 15.9 grams carbohydrate, 9.5 grams fat
> (1.4 saturated), 0 milligrams cholesterol,
> 715 milligrams sodium, 4.3 grams fiber

helpful hints

● *There are several jerk seasonings, liquid and dry, available. Choose whichever one suits your taste.*

● *If jerk seasoning is unavailable, make your own by mixing 1 teaspoon dried thyme, 1 teaspoon salt, 1/2 teaspoon allspice, 1/2 teaspoon cinnamon, and a pinch of cayenne pepper together.*

● *If you are really pressed for time, serve the jerk pork with a washed, ready-to eat salad and 2 tablespoons of no-sugar-added salad dressing instead of the palm heart salad.*

countdown

● *Assemble salad.*
● *Make Jerk Pork.*

shopping list

FRUIT AND VEG
  1 bag washed, ready-to-eat salad
  1 medium cucumber
  2 medium tomatoes
MEAT
  2 x (6-ounce) boneless pork chops
GROCERY
  1 (14-ounce) can hearts of palm
  1 small bottle jerk seasoning
STAPLES
  No-sugar-added oil and vinegar dressing
  Canola oil

Greek Shrimp with Feta Cheese **p127**

savory sage chicken

This is a tasty, 10-minute meal created by adding a quick sage and flour coating and a wine sauce to shop-bought roasted chicken.

savory sage chicken

1 tablespoon flour

2 teaspoons dried ground sage

Salt and freshly ground black pepper

2 (6-ounce) roasted boneless, skinless chicken breasts

1 tablespoon olive oil

¼ cup dry vermouth

¼ cup water

Mix together flour, sage, and salt and pepper to taste. Roll chicken in mixture, pressing flour into chicken on both sides. Heat a medium-sized nonstick skillet on medium-high heat. Add chicken to pan and cook for 1 minute per side. Remove to a plate and raise heat to high. Add vermouth and water and reduce for 2 minutes. Pour sauce over chicken.

Makes 2 servings.

Per serving: 383 calories, 54.5 grams protein, 4.1 grams carbohydrate, 14.9 grams fat (2.7 saturated), 144 milligrams cholesterol, 131 milligrams sodium, 0 grams fiber

italian zucchinis and tomatoes

¼ pound zucchini, sliced

2 medium tomatoes, cut into wedges about same size as zucchini

1 teaspoon dried oregano

2 tablespoons grated part-skim milk mozzarella cheese

Salt and freshly ground black pepper

Place zucchini and tomatoes in a microwave-safe bowl and microwave on high for 3 minutes. Add oregano, cheese, and salt and pepper to taste. Toss well.

Makes 2 servings.

Per serving: 74 calories, 6.5 grams protein, 9.6 grams carbohydrate, 2.1 grams fat (1.2 saturated), 7 milligrams cholesterol, 67 milligrams sodium, 0.9 grams fiber

helpful hints

● White wine can be substituted for vermouth.

● Roasted boneless, skinless chicken breasts come ready packaged in the the supermarket. Or use rotisserie-roasted chicken breasts.

● Dried oregano and sage are used in this recipe. Replace dried herbs after 6 months. If they look grey and old, that's probably how they will taste.

countdown

● Make Italian Zucchini and Tomatoes.

● Make Savory Sage Chicken.

shopping list

FRUIT AND VEG

  4 ounces zucchini

  2 medium tomatoes

DAIRY

  1 small package grated part-skim milk mozzarella cheese

MEAT

  2 X (6-ounce) roasted boneless, skinless chicken breasts

GROCERY

  1 small bottle dry vermouth

STAPLES

  Dried oregano

  Dried ground sage

  Flour

  Olive oil

  Salt

  Black peppercorns

which carb

super speed

suppers

swordfish in spanish sofrito sauce

This meal fits the nutritional guidelines for the Which Carbs phase.

Onions, garlic, green bell peppers, and tomatoes form the basis for a Spanish sofrito sauce. The Italian sofrito is similar using chopped celery, green peppers, onion, garlic, and herbs. It's used for soups and stews. Spanish sofrito can be bought in a jar or can in some supermarkets. If difficult to find, use a thick tomato salsa instead.

Brown rice takes about 45 minutes to cook. There are several brands of quick-cooking brown rice available. Their cooking time ranges from 10 to 30 minutes. The 10-minute rice is used in this dinner.

swordfish in spanish sofrito sauce

³/₄ pound swordfish

2 teaspoons olive oil

Salt and freshly ground black pepper

1 cup sofrito or thick no-sugar-added tomato salsa

Wash fish and pat dry with kitchen paper. Heat oil in a medium-sized nonstick skillet on medium-high heat and add fish. Brown for 2 minutes. Turn and brown second side for 2 minutes. Season cooked sides with salt and pepper. Lower heat to medium, add sofrito, cover, and simmer for 5 minutes for 1-inch thick fish, 3–4 minutes for ¹/₂-inch thick fish.
Makes 2 servings.

> Per serving: 308 calories, 33.6 grams protein, 0 grams carbohydrate, 12.8 grams fat (2.4 saturated), 66 milligrams cholesterol, 152 milligrams sodium, 0 grams fiber

yellow rice

1¹/₃ cups water

1¹/₃ cups 10-minute quick-cooking brown rice

¹/₂ teaspoon turmeric

¹/₄ cup diced or sliced sweet pimiento, drained

1 teaspoon olive oil

Bring water to the boil in a large saucepan over high heat. Lower heat to medium-high and add rice. Cover and cook for 5 minutes. Remove from heat and let stand for 5 minutes. Stir in pimiento and olive oil. Add salt and pepper to taste.
Makes 2 servings.

> Per serving: 196 calories, 5.0 grams protein, 36.0 grams carbohydrate, 3.9 grams fat (0.6 saturated), 0 milligrams cholesterol, 3 milligrams sodium, 2 grams fiber

helpful hints

● *Any meaty fish such as halibut or tuna can be used. This meal also works well with canned tuna.*

● *Saffron can be used instead of the turmeric in the rice.*

● *Look for: sofrito with 15 calories and 0.4 grams of fat per ounce.*

countdown

● *Start rice.*

● *Make swordfish.*

● *Assemble dessert.*

shopping list

SEAFOOD

³/₄ pound swordfish

GROCERY

1 jar sofrito or thick no-sugar-added tomato salsa

1 small jar turmeric

1 small jar diced or sliced sweet pimiento

STAPLES

Olive oil

10-minute quick-cooking brown rice

Salt

Black peppercorns

peasant country soup

This meal fits the nutritional guidelines for the Which Carbs phase.

This warm, hearty soup can be made in about 15 minutes. It keeps well. Make extra and freeze for another quick meal if you have the time.

peasant country soup

2 teaspoons olive oil

1 pound sliced button mushrooms

1 1/2 cups pasta sauce

3/4 cup fat-free, low-sodium chicken broth

3/4 cup water

3/4 cup cooked white navy or cannellini beans, rinsed and drained

1/4 pound roasted chicken strips or pieces

Salt and freshly ground black pepper

Heat olive oil in a medium-sized saucepan over high heat. Add mushrooms and sauté for 1 minute. Add pasta sauce, chicken broth, water, and beans. Bring to the boil and simmer for 10 minutes. Add chicken and cook for 1 minute to warm through. Add salt and pepper to taste. *Makes 2 servings.*

> Per serving: 334 calories, 29.7 grams protein, 33.6 grams carbohydrate, 8.7 grams fat (1.2 saturated), 48 milligrams cholesterol, 856 milligrams sodium, 6.2 grams fiber

herb cheese toast and salad

2 slices whole wheat bread

Olive oil spray

2 ounces herbed goat cheese

4 cups washed, ready-to-serve salad

2 tablespoons no-sugar-added oil and vinegar dressing

Pre-heat broiler. Spray whole wheat slices with olive oil spray and spread with goat cheese. Broil for 1 to 2 minutes until cheese is melted. Cut bread into 2 triangles. Place salad in a bowl and toss with dressing. Divide between 2 salad plates and place 2 toast triangles (1 slice) on the side. Serve with soup. *Makes 2 servings.*

> Per serving: 237 calories, 10.7 grams protein, 12.6 grams carbohydrate, 18.0 grams fat (7.1 saturated), 22 milligrams cholesterol, 342 milligrams sodium, 3.3 grams fiber

beef teriyaki with chinese noodles

This meal fits the nutritional guidelines for the Which Carbs phase.

Juicy beef in a spicy teriyaki sauce is a traditional Japanese dish. This one can be made in minutes by buying the teriyaki sauce and the vegetables already cut for stir-fry. Some supermarkets have the meat and vegetables cut and ready to use for stir-frying in one package. Or go to the salad bar section and buy the vegetables cut up there.

beef teriyaki

3/4 pound sirloin steak, cut for stir-fry
1 teaspoon sesame oil
1 cup sliced onion
2 garlic cloves, crushed
1/4 pound sliced mushrooms
1/4 cup lite teriyaki sauce

Cut beef into strips, 3 inches long and 1/4 inch wide, if not already cut. Heat sesame oil in a nonstick skillet or wok on high heat. Add onion, garlic, and mushrooms. Stir-fry for 2 minutes. Add beef and stir-fry for 1 minute. Add teriyaki sauce and continue to cook for 1 minute.
Makes 2 servings.

Per serving: 456 calories, 63.9 grams protein, 14.2 grams carbohydrate, 17.3 grams fat (7.6 saturated), 153 milligrams cholesterol, 755 milligrams sodium, 0 grams fiber

chinese noodles

1 cup fresh Chinese noodles or dried noodles
1 teaspoon sesame oil
6 scallions, sliced
Salt and freshly ground black pepper

Bring 2–3 quarts of water to the boil in a large saucepan over high heat. Add noodles and cook for 1 minute or according to package instructions. Drain. Add sesame oil, scallions, and salt and pepper to taste. Divide between 2 dinner plates and serve Beef Teriyaki on top.
Makes 2 servings.

Per serving: 167 calories, 5.0 grams protein, 27.6 grams carbohydrate, 4.0 grams fat (0.6 saturated), 33 milligrams cholesterol, 9 milligrams sodium, 1.1 grams fiber

helpful hints

● *Look out for 'lite' teriyaki sauce with 15 calories per tablespoon, 320 mg sodium and 3 grams carbohydrates.*
● *Canola oil can be used instead of sesame oil.*
● *Fresh Chinese noodles can be found in the fruit and veg section of the supermarket. Or dried noodles can be used.*
● *Angel-hair pasta can be substituted for the Chinese noodles.*
● *Beef topside can be used instead of sirloin.*

countdown

● *Boil water for noodles.*
● *Make Beef Teriyaki.*
● *Make Chinese Noodles.*

shopping list

FRUIT AND VEG
  1 small package sliced mushrooms (4 ounces needed)
  1 small bunch scallions
  1 small package fresh Chinese noodles or dried noodles
MEAT
  3/4 pound sirloin steak, cut for stir-fry
GROCERY
  1 small bottle sesame oil
  1 small bottle teriyaki sauce
STAPLES
  Onion
  Garlic
  Salt
  Black peppercorns

right carb

super speed

lunches

parmesan sole

This meal fits the nutritional guidelines for the Right Carbs phase.

Fish is the original fast food. It takes only minutes to cook. For this quick meal, grated Parmesan cheese and breadcrumbs top the sole. This entire meal can be put together in 15 minutes.

parmesan sole

Olive oil spray
3/4 pound sole fillet (1/2 inch thick)
2 teaspoons olive oil
2 tablespoons plain breadcrumbs
2 tablespoons freshly grated
    Parmesan cheese
Salt and freshly ground black
    pepper
2 small tomatoes, sliced

Pre-heat grill. Line a baking tray with foil and spray with olive oil spray. Rinse fish and pat dry. Place on tray and brush with 1 teaspoon olive oil. Grill for 5 minutes. Mix together breadcrumbs, Parmesan cheese, remaining oil and salt and pepper to taste. Remove sole from grill and place tomato slices over fish. Spread breadcrumb mixture evenly over fish. Grill for 2 minutes. Remove and serve.
Makes 2 servings.

> Per serving: 287 calories, 38.1 grams protein, 6.8 grams carbohydrate, 11.5 grams fat (3.4 saturated), 64 milligrams cholesterol, 300 milligrams sodium, 0 grams fiber

potato cubes

3/4 pound new potatoes
2 teaspoons olive oil
Salt and freshly ground black
    pepper

Wash, but do not peel, potatoes. Cut into 1-inch cubes. Place in a microwave-safe bowl and cover with plastic wrap or a plate. Microwave on high for 5 minutes. Remove and let stand, covered, for 1 minute. Remove cover carefully, because the steam will be very hot. Add olive oil and salt and pepper to taste. Toss well.
Makes 2 servings.

> Per serving: 180 calories, 3.5 grams protein, 3 0.6 grams carbohydrate, 4.7 grams fat (0.6 saturated), 0 milligrams cholesterol, 11 milligrams sodium, 2.7 grams fiber

dessert

3 cups melon cubes

Divide between 2 dessert bowls.
Makes 2 servings.

> Per serving: 86 calories, 2.1 grams protein, 20.1 grams carbohydrate, 0.6 grams fat (0 saturated), 0 milligrams cholesterol, 21 milligrams sodium, 0.8 grams fiber

helpful hints

- *Any type of delicate white fish fillet can be used such as snapper or flounder.*
- *Fresh melon cubes can be found in the fruit and veg section of most supermarkets.*

countdown

- *Pre-heat grill.*
- *Make potato cubes.*
- *Make Parmesan Sole.*
- *Assemble dessert.*

shopping list

FRUIT AND VEG
    3/4 pound new potatoes
    2 small tomatoes
    1 container melon cubes
        (about 1 pound)
SEAFOOD
    3/4 pound sole fillet
GROCERY
    Plain breadcrumbs
STAPLES
    Olive oil spray
    Olive oil
    Parmesan cheese
    Salt
    Black peppercorns

chicken creole

This meal fits the nutritional guidelines for the Right Carbs phase.

Green bell peppers and onions are essential ingredients of Creole and Cajun cooking. Add some tomatoes, hot peppers, and chicken and you've got a quick and easy Chicken Creole. The amount of cayenne called for in the recipe gives a mild zing to the sauce. If you like it hot, add more cayenne or serve hot pepper sauce at the table.

Brown rice takes about 45 minutes to cook. There are several brands of quick-cooking brown rice available. Their cooking time ranges from 10 to 30 minutes. The 10-minute rice is used in this recipe.

chicken creole

1 teaspoon olive oil

1½ cups frozen chopped onion

1 cup frozen diced green bell pepper

4 garlic cloves, crushed

2 cups no-sugar-added chopped tomatoes

2 teaspoons dried oregano

1 tablespoon Worcestershire sauce

⅛ teaspoon cayenne pepper

¾ pound roasted boneless, skinless chicken breast, cut into 1-inch cubes

Salt and freshly ground black pepper

Hot pepper sauce

Heat olive oil in a medium-sized nonstick skillet on medium-high heat and add onion, green bell pepper, and garlic. Sauté for 2 minutes. Add tomatoes, oregano, Worcestershire sauce, cayenne pepper, and chicken to pan. Simmer for 3 minutes. Add salt and pepper to taste. Spoon chicken and sauce over rice and pass the hot pepper sauce.

Makes 2 servings.

> Per serving: 436 calories, 59.1 grams protein, 28.1 grams carbohydrate, 10.5 grams fat (2.2 saturated), 144 milligrams cholesterol, 411 milligrams sodium, 4.6 grams fiber

helpful hints

- Look for roasted chicken breasts that have not been cooked in a honey, sugar, or barbecue sauce.
- Dried oregano is used in this recipe. Replace dried herbs after 6 months. If they look grey and old, that's probably how they will taste.
- Fresh watermelon cubes can be found in the fruit and veg section of some supermarkets.

countdown

- Boil water for rice.
- Make chicken dish and cover to keep warm.
- Make rice.
- Assemble the dessert.

quick brown rice

1 cup 10-minute quick-cooking
   brown rice
1 cup water
Salt and freshly ground black
   pepper

Bring water to the boil in a large saucepan over high heat and add rice. Boil for 5 minutes. Cover with a lid and let stand for 5 minutes. Or follow package instructions. Fluff with a fork and add salt and pepper to taste.

Makes 2 servings.

Per serving: 128 calories, 3.8 grams protein, 26.3 grams carbohydrate, 1.3 grams fat (0.2 saturated), 0 milligrams cholesterol, 0 milligrams sodium, 1.5 grams fiber

dessert

2 cups watermelon cubes

Divide between 2 dessert bowls.

Makes 2 servings.

Per serving: 49 calories, 1 gram protein, 11.1 grams carbohydrate, 0.7 grams fat (0.1 saturated), 0 milligrams cholesterol, 3 milligrams sodium, 0.8 grams fiber

shopping list

FRUIT AND VEG
   2 cups watermelon cubes
MEAT
   ³/₄ pound roasted boneless,
      skinless chicken breast
GROCERY
   1 pound can no-sugar-added
      chopped tomatoes
STAPLES
   Frozen chopped onion
   Frozen diced green bell
      pepper
   Garlic
   Cayenne pepper
   Dried oregano
   Worcestershire sauce
   Hot pepper sauce
   10-minute, quick-cooking
      brown rice
   Olive oil
   Salt
   Black peppercorns

black bean soup with rice

helpful hints

- If you like your black bean soup thick, remove about 1 cup of beans from the soup after it is cooked and purée them in a food processor. Stir the purée into the soup.
- Any type of hard grating cheese can be used.
- Brown rice takes about 45 minutes to cook. There are several brands of quick-cooking brown rice available. Their cooking time ranges from 10 to 30 minutes. Use the 10-minute rice for this dinner.

countdown

- Make rice.
- Make soup.

shopping list

DAIRY
  1 small package Manchego cheese
DELI
  6 ounces lean gammon
STAPLES
  10-minute, quick-cooking brown rice
  Chili powder
  Frozen chopped onion
  Frozen diced green bell pepper
  Olive oil
  Canned black beans (8 ounces needed)
  Fat-free, low-sodium chicken broth
  Salt
  Black peppercorns

This meal fits the nutritional guidelines for the Right Carbs phase.

This hearty black bean soup makes a quick one-pot dinner. Manchego is a flavorful, semi-firm Spanish cheese made from sheep's milk.

rice

$^2/_3$ cup 10-minute quick-cooking brown rice
$^2/_3$ cup water
Salt and freshly ground black pepper

Bring water to the boil in a large saucepan over high heat and add rice. Boil for 5 minutes. Cover with a lid and let stand for 5 minutes. Or follow package instructions. Fluff with a fork and add salt and pepper to taste.
Makes 2 servings.

Per serving: 85 calories, 2.5 grams protein, 17.5 grams carbohydrate, 0.8 grams fat (0.2 saturated), 0 milligrams cholesterol, 0 milligrams sodium, 1 gram fiber

black bean soup

1 tablespoon olive oil
6 ounces lean Canadian bacon, cut into 2-inch strips
1 cup frozen diced green bell pepper
1 cup frozen chopped onion
2 cups rinsed and drained black beans
1 cup fat-free, low-sodium chicken broth
1 cup water
1 tablespoon chili powder
Salt and freshly ground black pepper
$^1/_2$ cup grated Manchego cheese

Heat olive oil in a large saucepan on medium-high heat. Add the gammon, green bell pepper, and onion. Sauté for 1 minute. Add beans, chicken broth, water, and chili powder. Bring to a simmer and cook for 5 minutes. Add salt and pepper to taste. Sprinkle cheese on top. To serve, divide rice between 2 soup bowls and spoon soup on top.
Makes 2 servings.

Per serving: 555 calories, 41.8 grams protein, 54.0 grams carbohydrate, 19.4 grams fat (6.9 saturated), 65 milligrams cholesterol, 1100 milligrams sodium, 7.2 grams fiber

mock hungarian goulash

This meal fits the nutritional guidelines for the Right Carbs phase.

Succulent beef in a tomato sauce flavored with onion, green bell pepper, and paprika is the basis for Hungarian goulash. I've shortened this recipe by using good-quality, lean deli roast beef and called it Mock Hungarian Goulash. The secret to a good Hungarian goulash is good Hungarian paprika. Paprika is the Hungarian name for both sweet pepper and the powder made from it. Ordinary paprika comes in varying degrees of flavor – from pungent to virtually tasteless. True Hungarian paprika may be hot or mild and can be found in most supermarkets.

mock hungarian goulash

1 teaspoon olive oil

1/2 cup frozen chopped onion

1 cup frozen diced green bell pepper

1 cup sliced portobello mushrooms

1 tablespoon Hungarian paprika or 1 1/2 tablespoons paprika

1 cup low-sodium, no-sugar-added tomato sauce

6 ounces thick sliced lean deli roast beef, cut into 1/2-inch wide strips

Salt and freshly ground black pepper

2 tablespoons reduced-fat crème fraiche

2 medium tomatoes, cut into wedges

Heat oil in a medium-sized nonstick skillet on medium-high heat and add onion, green bell pepper, and mushrooms. Sauté for 1 minute. Sprinkle paprika over vegetables and sauté for 3 minutes. Add tomato sauce and simmer for 1 minute. Add roast beef and salt and pepper to taste. Remove from heat and serve over noodles. Spoon crème fraiche on top and arrange tomatoes on the side.

Makes 2 servings.

Per serving: 311 calories, 31.0 grams protein, 21.3 grams carbohydrate, 10.8 grams fat (4.0 saturated), 77 milligrams cholesterol, 100 milligrams sodium, 1.5 grams fiber

caraway noodles

1/4 pound flat egg noodles

2 teaspoons olive oil

1 tablespoon caraway seeds

Salt and freshly ground black pepper

Bring 2–3 quarts of water to the boil in a large saucepan over high heat. Add the noodles and boil for 3–4 minutes or according to package instructions. Drain, leaving about 2 tablespoons water with the noodles. Toss with oil and caraway seeds. Add salt and pepper to taste. Divide between 2 plates and spoon goulash on top.

Makes 2 servings.

Per serving: 228 calories, 6.7 grams protein, 34.8 grams carbohydrate, 6.6 grams fat (1.0 saturated), 46 milligrams cholesterol, 10 milligrams sodium, 1.5 grams fiber

helpful hints

● Look for thinly sliced mushrooms in the fruit and veg section of the supermarket. Any type of sliced mushrooms can be used.

● If Hungarian paprika is unavailable, use regular paprika. If you have it on hand, make sure it is a fresh jar. If your paprika is older than 6 months, it's time for a fresh jar.

countdown

● Boil water for noodles.
● Make goulash.
● Make noodles.

shopping list

FRUIT AND VEG

1 small package sliced portobello mushrooms (about 1 1/2 ounces needed)

2 medium tomatoes

DAIRY

1 small pot reduced-fat crème fraiche

DELI

6 ounces thick-sliced lean deli roast beef

GROCERY

1 jar Hungarian paprika or ordinary paprika

1 small jar caraway seeds

1/4 pound flat egg noodles

STAPLES

Olive oil

Frozen chopped onion

Frozen diced green bell pepper

Low-sodium, no-sugar-added tomato sauce

Salt

Black peppercorns

weekends

By noon on Fridays, I'm already looking forward to relaxing over the weekend and spending time with my family. I also look forward to meals on which I make a little extra effort, to make them special, but I don't want to slave over the stove all day preparing them. The recipes are full of flavor and intrigue. Just who could resist the idea of Adobo-Rubbed Cowboy Steak with Jalapeño Rice? Puts you into a good mood for watching a great movie on Saturday night. Though the rice does take a little time to cook, it doesn't involve you in a lot of work.

How to manage a blow-out weekend? No need to worry here. Remember, balance is the key. My husband has never found it difficult, even after a deviation, to return to the good-carb lifestyle, because the menus are so appealing and varied. Seasonal eating is ever-important. You will want fresh fish and light pasta dishes and salads in summer when the supermarket shelves are filled with a huge array of salads and vibrantly colored bell peppers, squashes and sweet vine-ripened tomatoes. In winter the more robust meats and hearty cabbage dishes provide warming, comfort food to tempt you to stay with the good-carb lifestyle.

The recipes in this section are still quick and easy, but they take a few extra minutes of preparation or contain special ingredients that you may not think of for week-night dinners. I've often made dinner party menus using these dishes and been asked for the recipes!

Garlic-Stuffed Steak is a fun weekend meal that meets the guidelines for the Quick Start section.

Chicken and Walnuts in Lettuce Puffs is a dinner with an Asian theme that fits the Which Carb Meal Plan. Asian flavors are all the rage now that we travel so much more widely in countries such as Laos, Vietnam, and Korea, and chefs in the West are experimenting with fusion dishes which can often be easily adapted to good-carb eating. The secret of staying with a good-carb lifestyle is providing enough variation in one's diet to satisfy the taste buds. Don't get bored or you may be tempted to stray.

Pan-Seared Tuna with Mango Salsa is a delightful blend of fusion flavors and styles that fits the Right Carbs phase. There is the opportunity to mix and match, but the meals have been created to achieve the nutritional priorities of that phase in your diet. My husband and I no longer think about what is and what isn't good-carb; we just consider it good food that fits into our busy schedules and is appreciated by our families.

And of course you can have desserts. Pears with Raspberry Coulis makes a refreshing end to a great Saturday evening feast.

All of the weekend meals in this section are incorporated in the 2-week plan for the appropriate phase.

quick start
weekend
meals

dijon chicken with crunchy couscous

The nutritional analysis for this recipes fits the Quick Start phase.

A tangy mustard sauce gently coats these chicken breasts. The couscous is made with lettuce, giving a crunchy texture to the couscous. We don't often think of cooking lettuce, but the French braise lettuce and use it to make soup.

dijon chicken

2 x (6-ounce) boneless, skinless
    chicken breasts

Olive oil spray

Freshly ground black pepper

1/2 cup dry vermouth

2 tablespoons Dijon mustard

2 tablespoons coarse-grain
    mustard

1 tablespoon whipping cream

Place chicken between 2 pieces of greaseproof paper and flatten with a kitchen mallet or the bottom of a heavy pan to 1/2-inch thick. Heat a medium-sized nonstick skillet on medium-high heat and spray with olive oil spray. Brown chicken for 2 minutes, then turn and brown second side for 2 minutes. Season the cooked sides with pepper to taste.

Remove chicken to a plate and add vermouth to the pan. Cook for 30 seconds, then add the two mustards and stir to blend, about 30 seconds. Return chicken to the pan and cook for 1 minute. Remove pan from heat and stir in the cream. Sprinkle over pepper to taste. Serve chicken on 2 dinner plates with the sauce spooned on top. *Makes 2 servings.*

> Per serving: 400 calories, 55.4 grams protein, 3.7 grams carbohydrate, 14.2 grams fat (4.2 saturated), 155 milligrams cholesterol, 859 milligrams sodium, 0 grams fiber

crunchy couscous

1 cup water

2/3 cup pre-cooked couscous

2 cups shredded iceberg lettuce

Salt and freshly ground black
    pepper

2 tablespoons sliced almonds

Several sprigs watercress, for
    garnish

Bring water to the boil in a medium saucepan on high heat. Add couscous and lettuce. Remove from the heat, cover, and let sit for 5 minutes. Fluff couscous with a fork and add almonds and salt and pepper to taste. Arrange sprigs of watercress on the side.
Makes 2 servings.

> Per serving: 146 calories, 5.8 grams protein, 18.4 grams carbohydrate, 6.2 grams fat (0.4 saturated), 0 milligrams cholesterol, 12 milligrams sodium, 2.1 grams fiber

helpful hints

- Four tablespoons of Dijon mustard can be used instead of the combination of Dijon and coarse-grain mustard.
- Any type of berry can be used for the dessert.
- Look for low-fat frozen yogurt with 240 calories, 6 grams fat and 40 grams carbs per 8 ounces. Some brands have fewer calories and less fat and carbs. Use whichever one you can find.

countdown

- Make couscous.
- Make chicken.
- Assemble the dessert just before serving.

shopping list

FRUIT AND VEG
  1 small head iceberg lettuce
  1 bunch watercress

DAIRY
  1 small pot whipping cream

MEAT
  2 x (6 ounce) boneless,
    skinless chicken breasts

GROCERY
  1 small bottle dry vermouth
  1 small jar coarse-grain
    mustard
  1 small package couscous
  1 small package sliced
    almonds

STAPLES
  Olive oil spray
  Dijon mustard
  Salt
  Black peppercorns

garlic-stuffed steak

The nutritional analysis for this recipes fits the Quick Start phase.
Garlic and parsley stuffed into a juicy steak make a perfect quick meal for the weekend.

The garlic cloves for this stuffing are blanched first and then chopped with fresh parsley to make a simple stuffing. Blanching gives the garlic a mild, sweet flavor. The water used for blanching the garlic has a wonderful flavor, so I add it to the water for cooking the pasta.

The asparagus is added for the last 5 minutes to the boiling pasta. This saves time and an extra pot to wash. If using fresh pasta, the cooking time will be about 3–4 minutes. Add the asparagus first and then the fresh pasta.

garlic-stuffed steak

5 garlic cloves, peeled
3/4 pound strip steak
1/2 cup chopped parsley
Salt and freshly ground black pepper
1 teaspoon olive oil

Place whole, peeled garlic cloves in a large saucepan and cover with cold water. Bring to the boil and scoop out garlic cloves with a strainer. Fill the saucepan with more cold water and bring to the boil for the pasta side dish.

Remove fat from steak and make slits about 1-inch apart on top and bottom to form pockets for the stuffing. The slits should be about 1/2-inch deep and cover the width of the steak.

Chop the garlic and parsley together. Add salt and pepper to taste. With the tip of a knife or a small spoon, stuff the slits in the steak using about half the parsley mixture. Set the rest of the stuffing aside. Heat a medium-sized nonstick skillet on medium-high heat and add the stuffed steak. Sauté for 5 minutes. Turn and sauté 5 minutes for rare. A meat thermometer should read 145 degrees. Cook 1–2 minutes longer for medium rare, or longer if you prefer your meat more well cooked. Season the cooked sides of steak.

Remove from the skillet to a chopping board and add the olive oil to the pan. Add remaining stuffing and sauté for 1–2 minutes. Cut the steak into 1-inch slices and divide between 2 dinner plates. Spoon sautéed stuffing on top of slices. Makes 2 servings.

Per serving: 397 calories, 61.5 grams protein, 3.6 grams carbohydrate, 17.1 grams fat (7.5 saturated), 153 milligrams cholesterol, 119 milligrams sodium, 0 grams fiber

Garlic-Stuffed Steak **p144–5**

linguine and asparagus

2 ounces whole wheat linguine

4 ounces asparagus

2 teaspoons olive oil

Salt and freshly ground black pepper

2 tablespoons grated Parmesan cheese

Bring a large saucepan with 2–3 quarts of water to the boil on high heat, using the garlic water from the stuffed steak recipe and additional water to make up the quantity. Add the pasta and boil for 5 minutes. Cut 1 inch from bottom of asparagus end and cut the asparagus spears into 1-inch slices. Add the asparagus to the pasta and continue to boil for 5 minutes.

Remove 2 tablespoons of the water and place in a large bowl. Drain the pasta and asparagus. Add olive oil and salt and pepper to taste to the water in the bowl. Add the drained pasta and toss well. Sprinkle with Parmesan cheese. *Makes 2 servings.*

Per serving: 179 calories, 8.7 grams protein, 20.4 grams carbohydrate, 7.9 grams fat (2.5 saturated), 7 milligrams cholesterol, 180 milligrams sodium, 4.3 grams fiber

helpful hints

- *Any herb can be used.*
- *Dried tarragon is called for in the recipe. If using dried herbs, make sure the jar is less than 6 months old.*
- *For best results, use a good-quality nonstick pan.*

countdown

- *Prepare ingredients.*
- *Complete omelette.*

shopping list

FRUIT AND VEG

  4 ounces asparagus

  1 small bunch parsley

MEAT

  3/4 pound strip steak

GROCERY

  1 small package whole wheat linguine (2 ounces needed)

STAPLES

  Garlic

  Olive oil

  Parmesan cheese

  Salt

  Black peppercorns

veal saltimbocca

The nutritional analysis for this recipes fits the Quick Start phase.

Saltimbocca means "jump in mouth," which perfectly describes this dish. Fresh veal scaloppini, an Italian staple, need only a few minutes cooking in a light wine sauce to flavor them.

veal saltimbocca

2 x (3-ounce) veal cutlets
Salt and freshly ground black
    pepper
2 thin slices lean ham (1 ounce)
4 small fresh sage leaves
2 teaspoons olive oil
¼ cup dry white wine
2 tablespoons water

Place veal on chopping board and season the side facing upwards. Lay one piece of ham on each piece. Cut each sage leaf into strips and place evenly on the ham. Roll up from the narrow end and secure with a wooden cocktail stick.

Heat the oil in a medium-sized nonstick skillet on medium-high heat. Add the veal rollups and sauté until brown on all sides, about 2 minutes per side. Add the wine, lower heat to medium, and gently simmer for 5 minutes.

Remove veal to 2 dinner plates and remove the cocktail sticks. Add water to skillet and reduce the liquid over high heat for 1 minute. Add salt and pepper to taste. Spoon sauce over veal.

Makes 2 servings.

Per serving: 263 calories, 25.2 grams protein, 0.4 grams carbohydrate, 14.3 grams fat(6.3 saturated), 82 milligrams cholesterol, 178 milligrams sodium, 0 grams fiber

helpful hints

● *Ask the butcher to flatten the veal for you. Or flatten it with the bottom of a heavy skillet or kitchen mallet.*

● *Veal may come in smaller pieces. Fill and roll in same manner, dividing filling among the pieces.*

countdown

● *Make Parmesan Zucchinis and Italian Salad*

● *Make Veal Saltimbocca.*

parmesan zucchinis

2 tablespoons grated Parmesan
  cheese
1/3 cup plain breadcrumbs
1/2 pound zucchinis, cut into
  1/2-inch slices
1 teaspoon olive oil
Salt and freshly ground black
  pepper

Pre-heat broiler. Mix Parmesan cheese and breadcrumbs together and set aside. Place zucchini slices in a shallow, microwave-safe bowl, cover, and microwave on high for 3 minutes. (Or bring a small saucepan filled with water to the boil. Add zucchinis and boil for 3–4 minutes. Drain and place in shallow baking dish.)

Drizzle olive oil and salt and pepper to taste over the zucchinis. Sprinkle with Parmesan mixture and place under broiler for 1–2 minutes or until topping is golden. *Makes 2 servings.*

Per serving: 128 calories, 5.2 grams protein,
12.2 grams carbohydrate, 5.8 grams fat
(2.3 saturated), 7 milligrams cholesterol,
281 milligrams sodium, 0.8 grams fiber

italian salad

4 cups washed, ready-to-eat
  Italian-style salad leaves
2 tablespoons no-sugar-added oil
  and balsamic vinegar dressing

Place salad in a bowl and add dressing.
Toss well.
Makes 2 servings.

Per serving: 87 calories, 0.8 grams protein, 2.3 grams
carbohydrate, 8.5 grams fat (1.3 saturated),
0 milligrams cholesterol, 83 milligrams sodium,
 0.4 grams fiber

shopping list

FRUIT AND VEG
  1 bag washed, ready-to-eat
    Italian-style salad leaves
  8 ounces zucchinis
  1 small bunch fresh sage
    leaves
DELI
  1 small package lean ham
    (1 ounce needed)
MEAT
  2 x (3-ounce) veal cutlets
GROCERY
  1 small bottle dry white wine
  1 small package plain
    breadcrumbs
  1 bottle no-sugar-added oil
    and balsamic vinegar
    dressing
STAPLES
  Parmesan cheese
  Olive oil
  Salt
  Black peppercorns

which carb

weekend

meals

adobo-rubbed cowboy steak

The nutritional analysis for this recipe fits the Which Carbs phase.

Texas cowboys working near the Rio Grande border loved their cowboy steaks flavored with Mexican spices. The spice mixture forms a crisp coating over the steak, keeping the meat juicy with a burst of flavor.

Brown rice takes about 45 minutes to cook. There are several brands of quick-cooking brown rice available. Their cooking time ranges from 10 to 30 minutes. I find the 30-minute rice has more flavor, but any quick-cooking rice will work for this dinner.

adobo-rubbed cowboy steak

1 teaspoon ground cumin
1 teaspoon ground ginger
1 teaspoon dried thyme
$1/8$ teaspoon cayenne pepper
2 medium garlic cloves, crushed
$3/4$ pound sirloin steak, fat removed
Olive oil spray
Salt

Pre-heat broiler. Line a baking tray with foil. Combine cumin, ginger, thyme, cayenne, and garlic in a bowl. Remove fat from steak. Spoon spice mixture over both sides of steak and press in with the back of a spoon. Spray both sides of steak with olive oil spray. Leave for 15 minutes while you prepare the rice.

Place steak on baking tray under broiler. Broil for 5 minutes. Turn and broil for 4–5 minutes for medium rare. A meat thermometer should read 145 degrees for rare. Broil a minute longer for a steak about 1-inch thick. Cook longer if you prefer your meat more well done. Sprinkle with salt to taste.

Makes 2 servings.

Per serving: 350 calories, 55.8 grams protein, 1.2 grams carbohydrate, 15.5 grams fat (7.2 saturated), 140 milligrams cholesterol, 104 milligrams sodium, 0 grams fiber

jalapeño rice

$1/2$ cup 30-minute quick-cooking brown rice
2 tablespoons olive oil and vinegar dressing
2 medium jalapeno peppers, seeded and chopped
2 scallions, thinly sliced
Salt and freshly ground black pepper

Bring a large saucepan with 2–3 quarts water to the boil. Add rice to the saucepan, stir once or twice, and let boil for 30 minutes. Alternatively, follow the cooking instructions on the rice package. Reserve 3 tablespoons cooking liquid and place in a serving bowl. Add the dressing to the bowl. Add peppers and scallions. Drain rice and add to bowl. Add salt and pepper to taste. Toss well.

Makes 2 servings.

Per serving: 237 calories, 5.2 grams protein, 34.3 grams carbohydrate, 9.8 grams fat (1.5 saturated), 0 milligrams cholesterol, 80 milligrams sodium, 1.5 grams fiber

helpful hints

● Any type of frying steak can be used.

● Dried thyme is used in this recipe. Replace dried herbs after 6 months. If they look grey and old, that's probably how they will taste.

countdown

● Pre-heat broiler and place foil-lined baking tray on top shelf.

● Start rice.

● Mix spices and garlic and marinate steak.

● Prepare remaining ingredients.

● Broil steak.

● Finish rice.

shopping list

FRUIT AND VEG
  2 medium jalapeño peppers
  1 small bunch scallions
MEAT
  $3/4$ pound sirloin steak (fillet or rump can be used)
GROCERY
  Ground ginger
STAPLES
  Ground cumin
  Dried thyme
  Cayenne pepper
  Garlic
  Olive oil spray
  30-minute quick-cooking brown rice
  Olive oil and vinegar dressing
  Salt
  Black peppercorns

mediterranean snapper with provençal salad

The nutritional analysis for this recipes fits the Which Carbs phase.

Sunny Provence with its abundance of fresh vegetables and herbs has a cuisine that is fragrant and simple.

The snapper recipe calls for one uncommon vegetable – fennel. It has a bulbous look, with wide, celery-like stems and bright green feathery leaves. It has a very light aniseed flavor. I used the feathery leaves as a garnish.

Pernod, an aniseed-flavored liqueur, is a perfect partner with fennel. You can buy small miniature Pernod bottles or use a dry vermouth instead.

provençal salad

1 tablespoon red wine vinegar
1 teaspoon Dijon mustard
1 teaspoon olive oil
¼ cup non-fat plain yogurt
Small head round lettuce,
    washed and dried
4 radishes, sliced
1 small green bell pepper, sliced
6 pitted green olives
2 small whole wheat rolls

Pre-heat oven to 350 degrees. Mix vinegar and mustard together in a salad bowl. Add oil and mix well. Blend in yogurt. Add lettuce, radishes, green bell pepper, and olives. Toss well. Warm rolls in oven while fish cooks.
Makes 2 servings.

Per serving: 145 calories, 7.9 grams protein, 20.8 grams carbohydrate, 5.2 grams fat (0.5 saturated), 1 milligram cholesterol, 493 milligrams sodium, 3.6 grams fiber

helpful hints

● *Any type of light white fish can be used. Cook the fish for 10 minutes per 1 inch of thickness.*
● *Any type of lettuce can be used for the salad.*
● *Two tablespoons of a no-sugar-added dressing can be used for the salad instead of the dressing in recipe.*
● *Cut off fennel stalks and slice using the thin slicing blade of a food processor or mandoline.*
● *A quick way to chop the fennel leaves is to snip them off the stalk with scissors.*

countdown

● *Make dessert*
● *Pre-heat oven to warm rolls.*
● *Make salad.*
● *Heat rolls.*
● *Make fish.*

mediterranean snapper

*³/₄ pound red snapper fillets
(about ¹/₂-inch thick)*
1 small bulb fennel, sliced
2 teaspoons olive oil
2 medium garlic cloves, crushed
¹/₄ cup Pernod
2 tablespoons whipping cream
*Salt and freshly ground black
pepper*

Rinse the fish and pat dry with kitchen paper. Remove top of fennel leaving only white bulb; wash feathery leaves and chop 2 tablespoons of leaves. Reserve some fennel ferns for garnish. Wash the fennel bulb and thinly slice. Heat the oil in a medium-sized nonstick skillet over medium-high heat. Add fennel slices and leaves, and garlic. Sauté for 3 minutes. Add fish and cook for 4 minutes per side. Remove fish to a plate and cover with foil to keep warm.

Add Pernod and reduce for 1 minute over high heat. Stir in cream and salt and pepper to taste. Spoon sauce with sliced fennel over snapper and sprinkle fennel ferns on top. *Makes 2 servings.*

Per serving: 374 calories, 35.3 grams protein, 1.5 grams carbohydrate, 12.8 grams fat (4.5 saturated), 83 milligrams cholesterol, 114 milligrams sodium, 0 grams fiber

pears with raspberry coulis

1 cup raspberries
*Sugar substitute equivalent to
2 teaspoons sugar*
2 medium pears

Place raspberries and sugar substitute in the bowl of a food processor and process until smooth. If you do not have a food processor, press berries through a sieve. Spoon sauce on to 2 dessert plates. Cut pears in half and remove core. Cut into slices and place on sauce. *Makes 2 servings.*

Per serving: 129 calories, 1.3 grams protein, 32.7 grams carbohydrate, 1.1 grams fat (0 saturated), 0 milligrams cholesterol, 1 milligram sodium, 7 grams fiber

shopping list

FRUIT AND VEG
  1 small bulb fennel
  1 small head round lettuce
  1 small bunch radishes
  1 small green bell pepper
  2 medium pears
  1 small package raspberries
DAIRY
  1 small pot non-fat plain
    yogurt
  1 small pot whipping cream
SEAFOOD
  ³/₄ pound red snapper fillets
GROCERY
  1 small container pitted
    green olives (6 needed)
  1 small pack whole wheat
    rolls (2 needed)
  1 miniature Pernod bottle
STAPLES
  Red wine vinegar
  Dijon mustard
  Olive oil
  Garlic
  Sugar substitute
  Salt
  Black peppercorns

chicken and walnuts in lettuce puffs

helpful hints

- Use toasted sesame oil if available in your local supermarket. It gives a smoky flavor.
- Chinese cabbage is also known as Chinese leaves. It has thin, crisp, pale green leaves. Any firm lettuce can be substituted.
- Hoisin sauce is a mixture of soybeans, garlic, chile peppers and spices. It can be found in the Chinese section of the supermarket.
- Rice vinegar can be bought in the Asian section of the supermarket. Half a tablespoon of water mixed with 1/2 tablespoon distilled white vinegar may be used as a substitute.

countdown

- Prepare walnuts and chicken.
- While chicken marinates, prepare all other ingredients.
- Stir-fry Sweet and Sour Cabbage.
- Using same wok, stir-fry the chicken dish.

The nutritional analysis for this recipes fits the Which Carbs phase.

Stir-fried chicken, walnuts, and vegetables served in lettuce puffs is one of my favorite dishes in a Chinese restaurant. Hoisin sauce spooned over crisp, cool lettuce and then topped with warm chicken and vegetables creates a taste and texture sensation.

I asked the chef at a top Chinese restaurant why cooking in a wok at home doesn't produce the same results as when food is prepared in a restaurant. Here's his advice: don't overcrowd the wok. Cook small portions. Use a wok that is about 20 inches in diameter; if using a smaller wok, use even smaller portions. Heat the wok until it is almost smoking, then add the oil. Drizzle the oil around the sides, swirling to coat the wok, and wait about 5 seconds before adding the other ingredients.

chicken and walnuts in lettuce puffs

1/4 pound boneless, skinless chicken breasts, cut into 1/2-inch pieces
1 tablespoon bottled oyster sauce
2 tablespoons walnut pieces
3 teaspoons sesame oil
1 teaspoon crushed fresh ginger or 1/2 teaspoon ground ginger
1 medium garlic clove, crushed
1/4 cup diced carrots
1/2 cup diced shiitake mushrooms
1/2 cup sliced water chestnuts
1/2 tablespoon rice vinegar
1/4 cup hoisin sauce
8 small iceberg lettuce cups (inner leaves from lettuce that curve into a cup)

Place chicken in a bowl with the oyster sauce and leave to stand for 10 minutes. Heat wok over high heat and add walnut pieces. Toast in wok for 1–2 minutes or until slightly colored. Remove and set aside. Heat wok over high heat. Add 1 teaspoon sesame oil. Add ginger and cook, stirring, until fragrant, about 10 seconds.

Add chicken and oyster sauce, and stir-fry for 1 minute. Add garlic, carrots, mushrooms, and water chestnuts. Stir-fry for 2 minutes. Add remaining 2 teaspoons sesame oil and rice vinegar. Cook to heat through for a few seconds. Add walnuts and toss to coat. Remove from heat.

To serve: divide chicken, hoisin sauce, and lettuce cups between 2 dinner plates. Spread a small spoonful of hoisin sauce on a lettuce cup, spoon in some of the chicken mixture, wrap in lettuce cup, and eat like a sandwich.
Makes 2 servings.

Per serving: 541 calories, 58.3 grams protein, 27.2 grams carbohydrate, 23.6 grams fat (3.6 saturated), 145 milligrams cholesterol, 797 milligrams sodium, 4.1 grams fiber

sweet and sour cabbage

Several drops hot pepper sauce

1 tablespoon hoisin sauce

2 tablespoons Chinese rice vinegar

Sugar substitute equivalent to
2 teaspoons sugar

1/2 teaspoon salt

1 teaspoon sesame oil

4 cups Chinese cabbage, thinly
sliced

1 medium red bell pepper, seeded
and sliced

Mix together hot pepper sauce, hoisin sauce, Chinese rice vinegar, sugar substitute, and salt. Heat wok to smoking and add sesame oil. When oil is smoking, add cabbage and red bell pepper. Stir-fry for 2 minutes. Pour in sauce. Toss well, spoon into a bowl, and leave to stand until chicken dish is ready. This can be served hot or cold. Do not wash the wok. It can be used for the chicken dish.

Makes 2 servings.

Per serving: 81 calories, 2.3 grams protein, 12.8 grams carbohydrate, 3.0 grams fat (0.4 saturated), 0 milligrams cholesterol, 691 milligrams sodium, 2.2 grams fiber

dessert

2 oranges

Slice oranges in quarters and place on 2 dessert plates.

Makes 2 servings.

Per serving: 62 calories, 1.2 grams protein, 15.4 grams carbohydrate, 0.2 grams fat (0 saturated), 0 milligrams cholesterol, 0 milligrams sodium, 3.1 grams fiber

shopping list

FRUIT AND VEG

1 small piece fresh ginger or
ground ginger

1 small package shiitake
mushrooms (2 ounces
needed)

1 small head iceberg lettuce

1 small head Chinese
cabbage (Chinese leaves)

1 medium red bell pepper

2 oranges

MEAT

4 ounces boneless, skinless
chicken breasts

GROCERY

1 small bottle oyster sauce

1 small bottle sesame oil

1 small bottle hoisin sauce

1 small can sliced water
chestnuts

1 small package walnut
pieces

STAPLES

Carrots

Garlic

Rice vinegar

Hot pepper sauce

Sugar substitute

Salt

steak in port wine

The nutritional analysis for this recipe fits the Which Carbs phase.

This typical French bistro dish is a delicious recipe and very simple to prepare. The shallots and mushrooms provide the base for the wine sauce.

Shallots have a milder flavor than onions. They are used in many sauces because their cellular structure allows them to melt into the sauce.

To flambé, if using gas, warm the cognac in the pan for a few seconds and then tip the pan so that the gas flame will ignite the liquid. Remove from the heat and wait for the flame to die down. If using an electric hob, throw a lighted match into the warmed cognac. When the flame dies down, remove the match. Keep a skillet lid nearby for safety.

Brown rice takes about 45 minutes to cook. There are several brands of quick-cooking brown rice available. Their cooking time ranges from 10 to 30 minutes. I find the 30-minute rice has more flavor, but any quick-cooking rice will work for this dinner.

helpful hints

- Beef tenderloin medallions or steaks may not be in the meat case. Ask the butcher to cut two 6-ounce beef tenderloin medallions for you. Or buy a 12-ounce piece of beef tenderloin and cut it into 2 steaks at home.
- Haricots vert or small French green beans can be found in most supermarkets. They are pencil thin and take only a few minutes to cook. If unavailable, use fresh green beans and cut into 2-inch pieces.
- To save washing another pan, use the same skillet for beans and steak.
- Slice mushrooms and shallots in a food processor fitted with a thin slicing blade.

countdown

- Start rice.
- Make beans.
- Make steak.

steak in port wine

1 teaspoon canola oil
2 x (6-ounce) beef tenderloin
  medallions
Salt and freshly ground black
  pepper
¼ cup cognac
5 medium shallots, peeled and
  thinly sliced
¼ pound portobello mushrooms,
  thinly sliced
¼ cup dry port wine
¼ cup fat-free, low-sodium
  chicken broth
2 tablespoons light cream
2 tablespoons chopped parsley

Heat oil in a nonstick skillet just large enough to hold the fillets in one layer over medium heat. Add the steaks and brown for 2 minutes, turn and brown 2 minutes more for a 1-inch thick steak. Add salt and pepper to taste to the cooked sides. If steak is 2–3 inches thick, lower the heat to medium and sauté the fillets 3 minutes for rare, 5–6 minutes for medium rare. Add the cognac to the steak and flambé.

Remove steak to a plate and cover with another plate or foil to keep warm. Add the shallots to the pan and sauté until golden, about 2 minutes. Do not let them turn dark brown or black. Add the mushrooms and sauté for 3 minutes. Add the port. Raise the heat to high and reduce the sauce for 1 minute. Add the chicken broth and reduce the sauce by half, about 1 minute. Stir in cream, and spoon sauce over steaks. Sprinkle with parsley.
Makes 2 servings.

Per serving: 470 calories, 38.6 grams protein, 11.7 grams carbohydrate, 19.0 grams fat (7.1 saturated), 115 milligrams cholesterol, 247 milligrams sodium, 0 grams fiber

brown rice

⅓ cup 30-minute quick cooking brown rice

Salt and freshly ground black pepper to taste

Bring a large saucepan with 2–3 quarts of water to the boil. Add the rice and boil for 30 minutes or according to package instructions. Drain and add salt and pepper to taste. Divide rice between 2 plates and place steak on top. Spoon sauce over steak and rice.

Makes 2 servings.

> Per serving: 85 calories, 2.5 grams protein, 17.5 grams carbohydrate, 0.8 grams fat (0.2 saturated), 0 milligrams cholesterol, 0 milligrams sodium, .0 gram fiber

french green beans

2 teaspoons canola oil

1 medium garlic clove, unpeeled

½ pound haricots vert (French green beans), trimmed

Salt and freshly ground black pepper

Heat oil in a nonstick skillet on medium-high heat. Add garlic and beans and sauté for 5 minutes or until beans are tender but firm. Remove garlic clove and add salt and pepper to taste.

Makes 2 servings.

> Per serving: 88 calories, 2.5 grams protein, 10.3 grams carbohydrate, 5.0 grams fat (0.6 saturated), 0 milligrams cholesterol, 4 milligrams sodium, 2.2 grams fiber

shopping list

FRUIT AND VEG
- 5 medium shallots
- 4 ounces portobello mushrooms
- 1 small bunch chopped parsley
- ½ pound haricots vert (French green beans)

DAIRY
- 1 small pot single cream

MEAT
- 2 x (6-ounce) beef fillet medallions

GROCERY
- 1 small bottle dry port wine
- 1 small bottle cognac

STAPLES
- Garlic
- 30-minute quick-cooking brown rice
- Canola oil
- Fat-free, low-sodium chicken broth
- Salt
- Black peppercorns

right carbs
weekend
meals

indian-spiced chicken

This fits the nutritional guidelines for the Right Carbs phase.

Tandoori chicken with its delicate blend of spices and intriguing aroma is cooked in a clay oven and heated by charcoal. All of the spices can be found in the supermarket.

indian-spiced chicken

³/₄ pound boneless, skinless chicken breasts

1 cup non-fat plain yogurt, drained

¹/₂ ounce fresh mint leaves plus 2 tablespoons, chopped

¹/₂ inch fresh ginger, peeled and chopped

1 teaspoon ground cilantro

Pinch cayenne

Sugar substitute equivalent to 2 teaspoons sugar

2 teaspoons canola oil

1 cup frozen chopped onion

2 medium garlic cloves, crushed

Salt and freshly ground black pepper

Remove fat from chicken and make 3 or 4 long slits in meat to allow marinade to penetrate. Mix yogurt, ¹/₂ ounce chopped mint, ginger, cilantro, cayenne, and sugar substitute together. Divide in half and reserve half the marinade in a separate bowl. Add chicken to half the marinade and let marinate for 10 minutes. Turn once during this time. Heat oil in a nonstick skillet just large enough to hold chicken in 1 layer over medium-high heat.

Remove chicken from marinade and discard marinade. Add onion, garlic, and chicken to the pan. Brown chicken for 3 minutes. Turn and brown for 2 minutes. Sprinkle salt and pepper to taste over cooked sides. Lower heat to medium. Spoon reserved marinade over chicken, cover, and cook for 5 minutes. A meat thermometer should read 160 degrees. Sprinkle with remaining 2 tablespoons mint and serve.

Makes 2 servings.

Per serving: 428 calories, 60.8 grams protein, 19.5 grams carbohydrate, 12.6 grams fat (2.5 saturated), 147 milligrams cholesterol, 223 milligrams sodium, 0 grams fiber

rice and spinach pilaf

1 teaspoon canola oil

1 cup frozen chopped onion

5 ounces spinach

¹/₂ cup basmati rice

1 cup fat-free, low-sodium chicken broth

¹/₂ teaspoon ground cumin

Salt and freshly ground black pepper

Heat oil in a medium-sized nonstick skillet on medium-high heat. Add onion and spinach. Sauté for 2 minutes. Add rice and sauté for 1 minute. Add chicken broth and cumin. When liquid comes to a simmer, lower heat to medium, cover, and simmer for 15 minutes. Remove from heat, add salt and pepper to taste and serve.

Makes 2 servings.

Per serving: 249 calories, 8.8 grams protein, 47.7 grams carbohydrate, 2.8 grams fat (0.4 saturated), 0 milligrams cholesterol, 368 milligrams sodium, 3.6 grams fiber

helpful hints

● *Fresh cilantro can be used instead of fresh mint. A quick way to chop mint is to snip the leaves off the stem with scissors.*

countdown

● *Marinate chicken.*
● *Start spinach and rice.*
● *Complete chicken.*
● *Complete rice.*

shopping list

FRUIT AND VEG

1 small piece fresh ginger

1 bag washed, ready-to-eat spinach (5 ounces needed)

1 small bunch fresh mint

DAIRY

1 small pot non-fat plain yogurt

MEAT

³/₄ pound boneless, skinless chicken breasts

GROCERY

1 small jar ground cilantro

1 small package basmati rice

STAPLES

Garlic

Canola oil

Fat-free, low-sodium chicken broth

Sugar substitute

Ground cumin

Frozen chopped onion

Cayenne pepper

Salt

Black peppercorns

- Pan searing requires that the skillet be very hot. Add the fish only when you see smoke rising from the pan.
- Use a nonstick skillet that is just large enough to hold the tuna.
- Peaches or plums can be substituted for mango.
- To cube mango, slice off each side of the mango as close to the stone as possible. Take the mango half in your hand, skin side down. Score the fruit in a criss-cross pattern through to the skin. Bend the skin backwards so that the cubes pop up. Slice the cubes away from the skin. Score and slice any fruit left on the stone.

countdown

- Make dessert 2 hours ahead.
- Make Saffron Pilaf.
- Make salsa.
- Make tuna.

pan-seared tuna with mango salsa

The nutritional analysis for these recipes fits the Right Carbs phase.

Pan searing is a perfect way to cook fish. The outside becomes crisp while the inside remains tender and moist. Toasting cumin and cilantro seeds in the skillet allows their natural oils to be released for a more concentrated flavor.

Brown rice takes about 45 minutes to cook. There are several brands of quick-cooking brown rice available. Their cooking time ranges from 10 to 30 minutes. The 10-minute rice is needed for this recipe.

The Lemon Chiffon is made with jelly and needs to be made at least 2 hours in advance. For a quick dessert, serve 1 orange per person.

pan-seared tuna with mango salsa

Salsa
1 ripe mango, cut into cubes
   (1/2 pound, about 1 cup)
2 tablespoons chopped red onion
1 teaspoon ground cumin
1 tablespoon balsamic vinegar
Several drops hot pepper sauce
1/4 cup chopped fresh cilantro
1 tablespoon cumin seeds
1 tablespoon cilantro seeds
1 teaspoon olive oil
3/4 pound tuna steak
Salt
2 whole wheat rolls

To prepare the salsa, combine mango, red onion, ground cumin, balsamic vinegar, hot pepper sauce, and cilantro in a bowl. Toss well. Taste for seasoning and add more cumin if needed.

To prepare the tuna, place cumin and cilantro seeds in a medium nonstick skillet over medium heat. Toss for 2 minutes and remove from heat. Place in a food processor or mini-processor and coarsely chop. Add olive oil and blend for a few seconds.

Rinse tuna and pat dry with paper towel. Spoon the spice mixture over both sides of the tuna, pressing the seeds into the fish with the back of the spoon. Heat the same skillet on high. It needs to be smoking before the tuna is added. Brown tuna for 1 minute on one side and turn. Brown for another minute and lower heat to medium-high. Cook for another 3–4 minutes. Add a little salt to taste. Remove tuna to 2 plates, spoon salsa on top, and serve with rolls.
Makes 2 servings.

Per serving: 322 calories, 37.2 grams protein, 19.6 grams carbohydrate, 10.3 grams fat (2.4 saturated), 59 milligrams cholesterol, 203 milligrams sodium, 1.1 grams fiber

saffron pilaf

1 teaspoon olive oil

1 cup 10-minute quick-cooking
   brown rice

1 cup water

1/8 teaspoon saffron

Salt and freshly ground black
   pepper

Heat olive oil in a medium nonstick skillet over medium heat. Add rice and sauté for 1 minute. Add water and saffron. Bring to a simmer and cover. Simmer for 15 minutes. Add salt and pepper to taste.

Makes 2 servings.

Per serving: 148 calories, 3.8 grams protein, 26.3 grams carbohydrate, 3.5 grams fat (0.5 saturated), 0 milligrams cholesterol, 0 milligrams sodium, 1.5 grams fiber

lemon chiffon

1 package sugar-free low calorie
   lemon jell-o gelatin

1/2 cup nonfat ricotta cheese

Make up jelly according to package instructions, using 6 large ice cubes instead of cold water for a quick set. Leave to set for 1 hour. Whip with a whisk, and fold in the ricotta cheese. Spoon into 2 glass dessert bowls or dishes and leave to set for 1 hour.

Makes 2 servings.

Per serving: 174 calories, 3.6 grams protein, 19.3 grams carbohydrate, 1 gram fat (0.3 saturated), 0 milligrams cholesterol, 236 milligrams sodium, 0.6 grams fiber

shopping list

FRUIT AND VEG

   1 bunch fresh cilantro

   1 ripe mango

DAIRY

   1 small pot low-fat ricotta
      cheese

SEAFOOD

   3/4 pound tuna steak

GROCERY

   2 whole wheat rolls

   1 small jar cumin seeds

   1 small jar cilantro seeds

   1 small package saffron
      threads

   1 package sugar-free, low
      calorie lemon jell-o gelatin

STAPLES

   Red onion

   Hot pepper sauce

   Balsamic vinegar

   Ground cumin

   Olive oil

   10-minute quick-cooking
      brown rice

   Salt

   Black peppercorns

pork chops with apple relish

The nutritional analysis for this recipe fits the Right Carbs phase.

Sweet and tart apple relish garnishes a sautéed boneless pork chop for this quick weekend dinner. This recipe calls for a Gala apple. It's a sweet, moderately crisp, juicy apple that holds its shape well and adds just the right amount of sweetness to the relish. If you can't find Gala apples, use another type of your choice.

You can buy boneless, butterflied pork chops in the supermarket. They have very little fat and cook quickly.

Shallots have a milder flavor than onions. They are used in many sauces because their cellular structure allows them to melt into the sauce.

pork chops with apple relish

1 teaspoon canola oil
2 x (6-ounce) boneless loin pork chops
Salt and freshly ground black pepper
1 medium Gala apple, cored and coarsely chopped
1 medium shallot, chopped
2 tablespoons apple cider vinegar
Sugar substitute equivalent to 2 teaspoons sugar

Heat canola oil in a small nonstick skillet over medium-high heat. Add pork chops and brown for 2 minutes. Turn and brown second side for 2 minutes. Season the cooked sides to taste with salt and pepper. Reduce heat to medium and cook for 4 minutes. A meat thermometer should read 160 degrees.

While pork chops cook, mix apple, shallot, apple cider vinegar, and sugar substitute together in a small bowl. Add salt and pepper to taste.

Place pork chops on individual dinner plates and spoon apple relish on top. *Makes 2 servings.*

Per serving: 325 calories, 45.5 grams protein, 12.7 grams carbohydrate, 10.1 grams fat (3.0 saturated), 146 milligrams cholesterol, 106 milligrams sodium, 1.9 grams fiber

toasted walnut lentils

1 cup fat-free, low-sodium chicken
    broth
1 cup water
½ cup dried lentils
2 tablespoons walnut pieces
Salt and freshly ground black
    pepper
¼ cup snipped chives

Bring chicken broth and water to a rolling boil in a medium-sized saucepan over high heat. Slowly add lentils so that the water continues to boil. Reduce the heat to medium-low, cover with a lid and simmer for 20 minutes. Meanwhile place walnuts on a foil-lined baking tray and toast in a toaster oven or under a broiler for several minutes. Watch them carefully. They burn easily. Remove lid and continue to cook lentils over high heat, until any remaining liquid has been absorbed. Season with salt and pepper to taste. Toss with walnuts and chives.
Makes 2 servings.

Per serving: 245 calories, 16.8 grams protein, 29.7 grams carbohydrate, 7.9 grams fat (0.7 saturated), 0 milligrams cholesterol, 285 milligrams sodium, 15.4 grams fiber

cranberry apple sauce

2 cups unsweetened apple sauce
2 tablespoons dried cranberries
¼ cup water

Divide apple sauce between 2 dessert bowls. Microwave cranberries with water for 1 minute. Drain cranberries, divide in half, and stir into the apple sauce.
Makes 2 servings.

Per serving: 145 calories, 0.4 grams protein, 42.1 grams carbohydrate, 0.2 grams fat (0.1 saturated), 0 milligrams cholesterol, 31 milligrams sodium, 4 grams fiber

shopping list

FRUIT AND VEG
    1 medium Gala apple
    1 medium shallot
    1 small bunch chives
MEAT
    2 x (6-ounce) boneless loin
        pork chops
GROCERY
    1 small bottle apple cider
        vinegar
    1 small package dried lentils
    1 small package walnut
        pieces
    1 small jar unsweetened
        apple sauce
    1 small package dried
        cranberries
STAPLES
    Canola oil
    Fat-free, low-sodium chicken
        broth
    Sugar substitute
    Salt
    Black peppercorns

entertaining

This section is geared to making parties that don't take all day to prepare. I love to have friends over, but find it hard to spend days shopping and cooking. I also want to serve food that's fun to eat and won't break the calorie bank. These parties let you splurge a little and still keep within the overall guidelines of the good-carbohydrate lifestyle.

They are designed for eight people to show you dishes you can make to follow a theme and create an atmosphere. The foods and quantities fit within the guidelines for the phase indicated at the top of each menu. You may want to make more and have some leftovers rather than run short (some guests may take more of a food they prefer and less of another).

Every detail of these parties has been planned for you including

- A shopping list with the amounts you will need
- A countdown for the days prior to and the day including the party

- The countdown indicates when to buy the ingredients, when to prepare each dish, and how to store and reheat or prepare them for serving.

Most of the recipes need very little preparation and many can be made ahead. There's almost no last-minute preparation.

Choose from the different party styles to best suit your occasion

- The Buffet for Friends is perfect for football or other sports-related parties, picnics or those times when you have a group over for a Sunday brunch after a family event.
- Prepare the Italian Supper for Friends for simple gatherings or casual Saturday nights. It is perfect for any season of the year.
- The Barbecue Party is easy to assemble, set up outside or in, and creates a fun atmosphere for your entertaining.
- It seems that a majority of guests want to hang out in the kitchen. So, serve the Casual Soup Supper right in the kitchen with the soup in a large pot on the

stove and the sandwiches and salad on the kitchen work surfaces.

- For the times you want an elegant dinner, the Dinner Party for Eight is your answer. Much of it can be made ahead and there are exact instructions for preparing the dishes so that you don't have to spend the evening in the kitchen.

Here are some general guidelines for drinks that will fit any of these parties:

- To keep within the good-carbohydrate guidelines, count 1 glass of alcohol or wine per person and choose from this list for some other interesting drinks for them to try.
- Make a jug of strong-flavored coffee, such as hazelnut or amaretto, and cool in the refrigerator. Serve over ice in tall attractive glasses. Be sure to place ice in the jug just before serving or serve the ice in a bucket on the side.
- Stay away from flavored syrups for coffee. They usually are made with a sugar syrup base.
- Make a jug of flavored iced tea such as peach, berry, or apple cinnamon. Or make a mixture of peach and apple cinnamon tea together. Set out glasses with a slice of the particular type of fruit in each glass.
- Serve no-sugar-added, flavored sparkling water with a twist of lemon or lime.

- Serve unusual-flavored diet soft drinks.

Decorate your table for the occasion. Let your table set the atmosphere and create a warm, welcoming feeling. A TV lifestyle expert gave me some tips on how to make your buffet table look attractive.

Decorate around the theme of the meal by using

- Italian pottery and colors for an Italian meal
- The colors of the teams playing for a sports party
- Colors from your garden for an outdoor party
- A tone-on-tone theme (for example, different shades of white and cream) for an elegant party.

Fill the buffet table with enticing objects. Take your colored napkins and go around the house looking for objects that go with them. Gather them together and see what looks best on the table. These can be pottery, vases, candlesticks, garden baskets, flowerpots, an old child's toy or a miniature wooden wheelbarrow. Select pieces that go with your theme or colors and set them on the table. Remove those that don't look right until you have an attractive display. Use these objects as bases for flower arrangements, napkin, and cutlery holders, or just as a design element on the table. This will make your table fun and inviting without having to spend hours preparing a groaning display of food.

italian supper
for friends

italian supper for friends

This party fits the guidelines for the Which Carbs section.

This Italian meal is perfect for a casual buffet. Most of the recipes can be made ahead, leaving just a few things to do on the day.

Menu

Garden Crudités and Dips

Chicken Tonnato

Lentil and Rice Salad

String Beans with Crumbled Gorgonzola

White Chocolate Whip

Countdown

Two days ahead

● Shop for ingredients.

One day ahead

● Poach chicken and make sauce.

● Cut zucchini for crudités, and store in plastic bags in the refrigerator.

● Make Lentil and Rice Salad and place in attractive bowl. Wrap and refrigerate.

● Blanch green beans, place in plastic bag, and refrigerate.

Morning of the party

● Make dessert, place in dessert glasses or dishes, and refrigerate.

● Slice fennel, arrange crudités platter, wrap, and refrigerate. Make dip.

● Arrange string beans on a platter, wrap, and refrigerate.

● Arrange chicken on platter with sauce, peppers, capers, and olives. Wrap and refrigerate.

One hour before guests arrive

● Remove finished dishes from refrigerator to bring to room temperature.

● Drizzle dressing on green beans and sprinkle cheese on top.

shopping list

Buy 2 days ahead of party

FRUIT AND VEG
  ½ pound broccoli florets
  1½ pounds haricots vert
    (small green beans)
  1 small zucchini
  2 medium fennel bulbs
DAIRY
  1 large carton nonfat plain
    yogurt
  30 ounces nonfat ricotta
    cheese
  1 package crumbled
    Gorgonzola
MEAT
  8 x (6-ounce) boneless,
    skinless chicken breasts
GROCERY
  1 small jar honey
  1 small package dried lentils
  1 small package basmati rice
  1 small container saffron
    threads
  1 package pinenuts
  1 small jar ground cilantro
  1 small bottle dry white wine
  1 small can anchovy fillets
  1 jar sweet peppers

1 jar capers
1 container pitted black
  olives (18 needed)
2 packages instant fat-free,
  sugar-free, white
  chocolate pudding mix
  (3 ounces needed)
1 small package semi-sweet
  chocolate
STAPLES
  Staples
  Olive oil spray
  Red onions
  Garlic
  Dijon mustard
  Fat-free, low-sodium chicken
    broth
  Reduced-fat mayonnaise
  Olive oil and vinegar dressing
  Olive oil
  Salt
  Black peppercorns
  Canned tuna packed in water

garden crudités

½ pound broccoli florets, washed and cut in half, if large

1 small zucchini, washed and sliced diagonally in ¼-inch slices

2 medium bulbs fennel, sliced

½ cup nonfat plain yogurt

2 tablespoons honey

2 tablespoons Dijon mustard

Arrange the vegetables on a platter or plate. Mix yogurt, honey, and mustard together and place in a small bowl. Or slice the top off a small red cabbage and hollow out the inside. Spoon the dressing into the cabbage and serve near the crudités. Makes 8 servings.

Per serving: 56 calories, 2.2 grams protein, 9.1 grams carbohydrate, 0.4 grams fat (0 saturated), 0 milligrams cholesterol, 110 milligrams sodium, 0.8 grams fiber

helpful hints

● *If you can find one, use a yellow zucchini for extra color.*

● *Any type of pre-cut vegetables can be added.*

● *Use cut vegetables from the salad bar. Pick and choose the vegetables that are in season.*

● *To slice fennel, cut off stem and leaves and slice the bulb only.*

chicken tonnato

helpful hints

● The chicken can be poached and the sauce can be made the day before and refrigerated.

● Save and freeze the remaining poaching liquid. It makes a wonderful broth for other recipes.

This is a traditional summer Italian dish that is perfect for buffets. The secret to keeping the chicken moist is to gently poach it and let it cool in the poaching liquid.

8 x (6-ounce) boneless, skinless chicken breasts

1/2 cup dry white wine

1 cup fat-free, low-sodium chicken broth

Salt and freshly ground black pepper

6 anchovy fillets

1 1/2 cups canned tuna, packed in water

2/3 cup reduced-fat mayonnaise

2/3 cup non-fat plain yogurt

1 1/2 teaspoons lemon juice

2 large bell peppers, thinly sliced

6 tablespoons capers, drained and rinsed

18 pitted black olives, halved

Remove fat from chicken. Add wine and chicken broth to a large saucepan. Bring to the boil on medium-high heat. Add chicken and then enough warm water to make sure all of the chicken is covered by liquid. Bring to a simmer, lower heat to medium-low, and gently simmer, uncovered, for 5 minutes. Do not boil the chicken. Remove from heat and let chicken cool in the liquid for 15 minutes (reserve 1/2 cup of the poaching liquid). Sprinkle chicken with salt and pepper to taste.

While chicken cools, make the sauce. Rinse anchovy fillets and place in the bowl of a food processor with tuna, mayonnaise, and yogurt. Process until smooth. Add poaching liquid and continue to process. Add lemon juice and process to blend into sauce.

To serve, remove chicken from liquid and place on serving platter. Spoon enough sauce over chicken to coat. Serve remaining sauce on the side. Lay pimiento strips across chicken. Sprinkle capers over chicken and arrange the olives attractively. Cover and refrigerate until needed. Bring to room temperature before serving.

Per serving: 412 calories, 59.9 grams protein, 6.8 grams carbohydrate, 17.2 grams fat (3.4 saturated), 153 milligrams cholesterol, 1057 milligrams sodium, 0.7 grams fiber

lentil and rice salad

2 cups fat-free, low-sodium
   chicken broth

2 cups water

1 cup lentils, rinsed to remove
   stones

$^2/_3$ cups basmati rice, rinsed

$^1/_4$ teaspoon saffron threads

Salt and freshly ground black
   pepper

$^1/_2$ cup pinenuts

$1^1/_2$ cups sliced red onion

6 garlic cloves, crushed

$^3/_4$ teaspoon ground cilantro

2 tablespoons plus 2 teaspoons
   olive oil

Bring chicken broth and 1 cup water to the boil in a nonstick pan on medium-high heat. Add the lentils slowly so that the broth continues to boil. Lower heat to medium. Cover with a lid and simmer for 5 minutes. Add rice, saffron, and remaining water to the lentils. Bring back to a simmer, cover, and simmer for 15 minutes. The liquid will be absorbed and the lentils cooked through, but firm. Add salt and pepper to taste.

While lentils and rice cook, heat a nonstick frying pan on medium-high heat and add the pinenuts. Sauté pinenuts for 1–2 minutes or until golden. Be careful because the nuts burn easily. Remove and set aside. Heat 2 teaspoons olive oil in the same pan and add the onion. Sauté, without browning, for 5 minutes. Add the garlic and continue to sauté for another 5 minutes.

Place lentils, rice, and onion in a large bowl and add the remaining 2 tablespoons oil, cilantro, and salt and pepper to taste. Toss well. Taste for seasoning and add more salt and pepper, if needed. Sprinkle toasted pinenuts on top and serve.

Makes 8 servings.

Per serving: 231 calories, 9.2 grams protein, 29.6 grams carbohydrate, 5.1 grams fat (0.7 saturated), 0 milligrams cholesterol, 144 milligrams sodium, 7.3 grams fiber

helpful hints

● *Turmeric can be substituted for the saffron.*

string beans with crumbled gorgonzola

1½ pounds haricots vert (small green beans)

3 tablespoons olive oil and vinegar dressing

Salt and freshly ground black pepper

4 ounces crumbled Gorgonzola

Bring a medium-sized saucepan of water to the boil. Trim beans and add to boiling water. As soon as the water comes back to the boil, drain and plunge beans into a bowl of iced water. Drain. Place on platter, drizzle dressing over the top and toss. Add salt and pepper to taste. Sprinkle cheese on top.

Makes 8 servings.

Per serving: 64 calories, 3.5 grams protein, 5.1 grams carbohydrate, 3.6 grams fat (2.1 saturated), 10 milligrams cholesterol, 194 milligrams sodium, 1.1 grams fiber

white chocolate whip

3²/₃ pounds nonfat ricotta cheese

2 cups water

½ cup fat-free, sugar-free instant white chocolate pudding powder

4 teaspoons grated semi-sweet chocolate

Whisk ricotta cheese and water together until smooth. This can be done in a food processor. Add the white chocolate pudding powder and whisk until smooth. Divide between 8 dessert bowls. Sprinkle ½ teaspoon grated chocolate on top of each dish.

Makes 8 servings.

Per serving: 114 calories, 0.1 grams protein, 4.9 grams carbohydrate, 0.2 grams fat (0.1 saturated), 0 milligrams cholesterol, 272 milligrams sodium, 0 grams fiber

dinner party
for eight

dinner party for eight

This dinner party fits the nutritional guidelines for the Which Carbs phase.

No need to spend all day making an elegant dinner party. These recipes are easy to make and you and your guests can enjoy the evening without worrying about the calories and carbs.

Menu

Bruschetta

Game Hens in Red Wine

Brown Rice with Toasted Pinenuts

Roasted Asparagus with Red Bell Pepper

Radicchio, Endive, and Watercress Salad

Berry Cups with Almond Sauce

Countdown

Two days ahead

- Shop for ingredients.

One day ahead

- Make Game Hens in Red Wine. Place in ovenproof casserole or dish in their sauce. Cover and refrigerate.
- Make Brown Rice with Toasted Pinenuts. Place in an oven-to-table dish, cover, and refrigerate.
- Make Almond Sauce for dessert. Cover and refrigerate.

Morning of the party

- Assemble berry cups without sauce and wrap and refrigerate.
- Prepare asparagus ready for the oven. Cut off the woody ends, place on baking trays, roll in olive oil, and place in refrigerator.
- Wash watercress, radicchio, and endive; dry and place in salad bowl. Cover with plastic wrap and refrigerate.
- Make bruschetta topping and refrigerate.

One hour before guests arrive

- Remove game hens, rice, asparagus, berries, and sauce from refrigerator.

Thirty minutes before guests arrive

- Pre-heat oven to 300 degrees.
- Place game hens in their sauce and rice in oven for 30 minutes to warm through.
- Remove salad from refrigerator and toss with dressing.
- Spoon topping for bruschetta on toasts and arrange on serving tray.

Before dessert

- Spoon sauce over berries just before serving.

shopping list

Buy 2 days ahead of party

FRUIT AND VEG

1 medium tomato

1 medium head radicchio

2 medium heads Belgian
endive

1 bunch watercress

2 pounds asparagus

3/4 pound button
mushrooms

1 package broccoli florets
(10 ounces needed)

Mixture of raspberries,
strawberries, and
blueberries (2½ pounds
berries needed)

DAIRY

1 carton reduced-fat crème
fraiche (12 ounces
needed)

MEAT

4 game hens, about
2 pounds each

GROCERY

1 jar sweet peppers (16
ounces needed)

1 package sliced almonds

1 package pinenuts

1 bottle almond essence

1 bottle red wine (Beaujolais
or Burgundy)

STAPLES

30-minute quick-cooking
brown rice

Olive oil spray

Red onion

Yellow onion

Carrots

Garlic

Whole wheat bread

Fat-free, low-sodium chicken
broth

Olive oil

Balsamic vinegar

Olive oil and vinegar dressing

Sugar substitute

Salt

Black peppercorns

bruschetta

Olive oil spray
1 cup sliced red onion
2 garlic cloves, crushed
1 medium tomato, diced
½ tablespoon olive oil
1 teaspoon balsamic vinegar
Salt and freshly ground black
*   pepper*
4 slices of whole wheat toast, cut
*   into squares*

Heat a nonstick skillet on medium-high heat. Spray with olive oil spray and add onion and garlic. Sauté for 10 minutes. The onion should be golden. Remove from heat and toss with tomatoes. Add olive oil, balsamic vinegar, and salt and pepper to taste. Place in a bowl and refrigerate until needed.

To serve, spoon tomato mixture on to toast and place on serving platter.

Per serving: 56 calories, 1.6 grams protein, 7.9 grams carbohydrate, 1.9 grams fat (0.4 saturated), 0 milligrams cholesterol, 39 milligrams sodium, 0.5 grams fiber

helpful hints

● *Belgian endive should not be placed in water to clean. The leaves will turn brown. Just remove any damaged outer leaves and then wipe with damp kitchen paper.*

radicchio, endive, and watercress salad

1 medium head radicchio
1 bunch watercress
2 medium heads Belgian endive
5 tablespoons olive oil and vinegar
*   dressing*

Wash radicchio and watercress and dry. Cut about 1 inch off flat end of endive and remove any torn or brown outer leaves. Wipe endive with damp kitchen paper. Tear radicchio leaves into bite-sized pieces. Break large stems off watercress. Slice endive into 1-inch circles. When salad is dry, place in a salad bowl, cover with plastic wrap, and refrigerate. Just before serving, toss with the dressing.
Makes 8 servings.

Per serving: 56 calories, 0.7 grams protein, 1.9 grams carbohydrate, 5.4 grams fat (1.9 saturated), 0 milligrams cholesterol, 59 milligrams sodium, 0.2 grams fiber

game hens in red wine

helpful hints

● Ask butcher to cut the game hens in half.
● You will need two 12-inch nonstick skillets to hold the birds in 1 layer. Or cook them in 2 batches.
● Slice vegetables in a food processor fitted with a slicing blade.

4 game hens, about 2 pounds each
Olive oil spray
2 cups diced yellow onion
2 medium carrots, diced
4 medium garlic cloves, crushed
1⅓ cups red wine (Beaujolais or Burgundy)
1⅓ cups fat-free, low-sodium chicken broth
4 cups sliced button mushrooms
Salt and freshly ground black pepper

Remove the fat from the cavity of the game hens and split them in half. Heat 2 large nonstick skillets just large enough to hold the halves in 1 layer over medium-high heat. Spray with olive oil spray. Brown the birds on both sides, about 5 minutes. Remove to a plate and pour off any excess fat.

Add the diced onion, carrots, and garlic to the pan. Sauté until the vegetables start to shrivel, about 5 minutes. Return game hen halves to the pan, lower the heat to medium, and cover with a lid. Leave to cook until the guinea fowl are cooked through, about 20 minutes. A meat thermometer should read 170 degrees for white meat and 180 degrees for dark meat.

Remove birds to a dish and cover with foil to keep warm. Pour off any remaining fat, add wine, and scrape the brown bits from the bottom of the pan while the wine simmers for about 2 minutes. Add the chicken broth and mushrooms. Simmer for 2 more minutes.

Remove skin from game hens and add salt and pepper to taste. If serving immediately, return the birds to the pan and let cook to warm through. Or place in an ovenproof serving platter and spoon sauce and vegetables on top. Cover and refrigerate. Remove from refrigerator and allow to come to room temperature, about 30 minutes. Place, covered with foil or a lid, in a 300 degrees oven for 20–30 minutes or until warmed through.

Makes 8 servings.

Per serving: 260 calories, 35.2 grams protein, 7.0 grams carbohydrate, 6.3 grams fat (1.6 saturated), 153 milligrams cholesterol, 215 milligrams sodium, 0.2 grams fiber

brown rice with toasted pinenuts

1 cup 30-minute quick-cooking
  brown rice

4 cups broccoli florets

3 tablespoons pinenuts

1 tablespoon olive oil

Salt and freshly ground black
  pepper

Fill a large saucepan with 2–3 quarts cold water. Add rice, cover with a lid, and bring to a boil over high heat. When water comes to the boil, remove the lid, lower heat to medium-low, and boil for 25 minutes. Add broccoli and continue to boil for 5 minutes. While rice boils, place pinenuts on a foil-lined baking tray and toast under a broiler for 2–3 minutes or until golden. Be careful because the pinenuts burn easily. When rice is cooked through, drain and toss with oil and salt and pepper to taste. Place in a serving bowl and sprinkle pinenuts on top.

Recipe may be made ahead until this point. Place rice in oven-to-tableware dish and store in the refrigerator. Before serving, bring to room temperature and place in pre-heated oven with guinea fowl for 30 minutes. Remove from oven and serve.

Makes 8 servings.

Per serving: 104 calories, 3.2 grams protein, 15.5 grams carbohydrate, 2.6 grams fat (0.4 saturated), 0 milligrams cholesterol, 10 milligrams sodium, 1.4 grams fiber

- *Asparagus takes only about 10 minutes in oven – roasting intensifies the flavor. Place in oven just before serving.*

roasted asparagus with red bell peppers

½ tablespoon olive oil

Salt and freshly ground black pepper

2 pounds asparagus

2 cups red peppers, cut in ½ inch pieces

Pre-heat oven to 400 degrees. Line a baking tray with foil and spoon oil on to foil. Add salt and pepper to taste. Add asparagus and roll in oil, making sure all spears are coated with oil and salt and pepper. Spread asparagus out to form 1 layer and roast in oven for 5 minutes. Remove asparagus and turn. Roast 10 more minutes for thick spears, 5 more minutes for thin ones. Remove from oven and arrange spears in straight rows on an oval serving platter. Cut peppers into thin strips and sprinkle over top. *Makes 8 servings.*

Per serving: 33 calories, 2.0 grams protein, 5.0 grams carbohydrate, 1.1 grams fat (0.2 saturated), 0 milligrams cholesterol, 8 milligrams sodium, 2.4 grams fiber

berry cups with almond sauce

8 cups berries (mixture of
  raspberries, blueberries, and
  strawberries)

2 teaspoons almond essence

Sugar substitute equivalent to 2
  teaspoons sugar

1 cup reduced-fat crème fraiche

3 tablespoons sliced almonds

Place berries in 8 small ramekins. Mix almond essence and sugar substitute into crème fraiche and spoon or dollop sauce on top of each one. Sauté almonds in a skillet until just turning golden. Be careful toasting the almonds as they burn easily. Sprinkle almonds on top of sauce. *Makes 8 servings.*

Per serving: 134 calories, 3 grams protein, 17.3 grams carbohydrate, 6.8 grams fat (2.7 saturated), 15 milligrams cholesterol, 20 milligrams sodium, 6.3 grams fiber

casual soup
supper

casual soup supper

This meal fits the nutritional guidelines for the Right Carbs phase.

Whenever we have friends over, it seems that everyone ends up standing around the kitchen. I planned this party so that the kitchen is part of the fun. I make the soup and leave it in a large, colorful saucepan on the stove with a ladle in the soup. The bowls are nearby and people can help themselves. The sandwiches and salad are placed on the work surface. Everyone can help themselves on their way to finding a seat at the table.

Menu

Creamy Wild Mushroom Soup

Broiled Grouper Sandwich

Three Bean Salad

Mango Fool

Countdown

Two days ahead

- Shop for most ingredients except the fish.

One day ahead

- Make soup, cover, and refrigerate.

Morning of the party

- Buy fish.
- Make Mango Fool, place in attractive glass, and refrigerate.
- Make salad. Place in serving bowl. Cover and refrigerate.

One hour ahead

- Prepare ingredients for grouper sandwich.
- Remove salad from refrigerator.
- Remove soup from refrigerator.

Fifteen minutes before guests arrive

- Marinate fish.

When guests arrive

- Place soup on stove and heat. When soup is hot, lower heat to extra low and leave until served.
- Make grouper sandwich just before serving.
- Remove dessert from refrigerator.
- Spoon sauce over berries just before serving.

shopping list

*Buy 2 days ahead of party
except seafood*

FRUIT AND VEG
1 bunch fresh dill
1 bunch scallions
   (6 needed)
3/4 pound sliced portobello
   mushrooms
2 medium tomatoes
1 medium Spanish onion
1/2 pound green beans
1/2 pound yellow beans
2 medium ripe mangoes
   (1 pound)
1 bunch fresh mint

DAIRY
1 small carton heavy cream
   (4 ounces needed)
4 pots nonfat, sugar-free
   mango or tropical fruit
   yogurt (32 ounces
   needed)

GROCERY
1 small package dried cèpes
   (mushrooms)

SEAFOOD
8 X (6-ounce) grouper fillets
   (purchase on the day of
   the party)

STAPLES:
Red kidney beans (18 ounces
   needed)
Yellow onion
Olive oil spray
Balsamic vinegar
Olive oil and vinegar dressing
Flour
Grated nutmeg
Multigrain bread
Fat-free, low-sodium chicken
   broth
Mayonnaise
Lemons
Salt
Black peppercorns

creamy wild mushroom soup

Many "wild" mushrooms are cultivated and don't have a strong flavor of the woods. Dried cèpes (called porcini in Italy) that have been gathered in the woods add a depth of flavor to this soup.

The secret to this soup is cooking the onion until it is sweet. Grated nutmeg gives the soup an intriguing flavor.

1/2 cup dried cèpe mushrooms

5 cups hot water

Olive oil spray

1 large yellow onion, sliced

3/4 pound sliced portobello mushrooms

1 tablespoon flour

4 cups fat-free, low-sodium chicken broth

8 tablespoons heavy cream

1/2 teaspoon grated nutmeg

Salt and freshly ground black pepper

Add dried cèpes to 1 cup hot water and leave to stand for 5 minutes. Drain, reserving the liquid, and slice. Strain liquid 2 to 3 times to remove sand.

Heat a large saucepan over medium-high heat and spray with olive oil spray. Add the onion and sauté for 2 minutes. Reduce heat to medium and continue to cook onion until golden, about 5 minutes. Do not brown onion. Add the portobello mushrooms and sauté for 2 minutes, stirring 1 or 2 times. Sprinkle flour on top and stir until absorbed, about 1 minute. Add chicken broth and remaining water. Lift reconstituted mushrooms from the hot water with a slotted spoon and add to the soup. Place a piece of paper towel in a sieve and strain the mushroom liquid into the soup. Bring to a boil. Simmer for 10 minutes. Add nutmeg and salt and pepper to taste.

Remove 1 cup soup to a blender or food processor and purée. Return to the soup. Spoon cream into soup and mix well. Taste for seasoning, adding more if necessary.
Makes 8 servings.

Per serving: 102 calories, 2.9 grams protein, 5.4 grams carbohydrate, 7.4 grams fat (3.8 saturated), 21 milligrams cholesterol, 288 milligrams sodium, 0 grams fiber

helpful hints

● *Slice onion and mushrooms in a food processor fitted with a 1/4-inch slicing blade.*

● *Cook the onion until it is transparent, but not brown, to give the soup a sweet flavor.*

● *Morel mushrooms can be substituted.*

● *The soup can be made a day in advance. It will thicken on standing. Stir in a little broth when reheating.*

grilled grouper sandwich

Grilling fish gives great flavor. Grill on a barbecue, use your kitchen broiler or simply sauté the fish in a skillet. A renowned fish chef once showed me this method for grilling fish in advance. Sear the fish on the grill about 1 hour before needed and then place in a 275 degrees oven to finish cooking for about 30 minutes. For a 1-inch thick fillet, sear 2 minutes per side and then place in oven.

helpful hints

- *Ask for the skin to be removed when you buy the fish.*
- *A quick way to chop dill is to snip the leaves with scissors.*
- *Make sure the grill bars are clean and spray them with vegetable cooking spray before grilling the fish.*

Any type of firm, white, non-oily fish fillet can be used.

8 x (6-ounce) grouper fillets
2 cups balsamic vinegar
$\frac{1}{2}$ cup mayonnaise
2 tablespoons lemon juice
1$\frac{1}{2}$ cups snipped fresh dill
Salt and freshly ground black
  pepper
16 slices multigrain bread
8 slices Spanish onion
8 slices tomato

Pre-heat grill. Rinse fish fillets and pat dry with kitchen paper. Place in a self-seal plastic bag and add balsamic vinegar. Marinate for 15 minutes. Meanwhile, mix mayonnaise with lemon juice and fold in 1 cup dill, reserving the rest for garnish. Add salt and pepper to taste.

Remove fish from bag and pat dry with kitchen paper. Place on a barbecue grill 4 inches from heat or under pre-heated kitchen broiler. Grill for 2 minutes per side. Season cooked sides. While fish is cooking, toast the bread.

To serve, spread each slice of toast with a layer of mayonnaise. Place a fish fillet on each slice. Place onion slices on the fish and finish with tomato slices. Sprinkle with reserved dill. Serve as open sandwiches.

Makes 8 servings.

Per serving: 455 calories, 36.8 grams protein,
38.9 grams carbohydrate, 14.7 grams fat
(2.5 saturated), 62 milligrams cholesterol,
570 milligrams sodium, 1.2 grams fiber

three bean salad

3 cups green beans, trimmed and
   cut into 1-inch pieces
3 cups yellow beans, trimmed and
   cut into 1-inch pieces
2 cups cooked red kidney beans,
   rinsed and drained
6 scallions, sliced
6 tablespoons olive oil and vinegar
   dressing
Salt and freshly ground black
   pepper

Bring a large saucepan filled with water to the
boil. Add the green and yellow beans. As soon
as the water returns to the boil, drain and refresh
under ice cold water. Place in a large serving
bowl and add the kidney beans, scallions, and
dressing. Toss well. Add salt and pepper to
taste. Toss once more.
Makes 8 servings.

Per serving: 141 calories, 4.4 grams protein,
17.1 grams carbohydrate, 6.7 grams fat
(1.0 saturated), 0 milligrams cholesterol, 61 milligrams
sodium, 2.2 grams fiber

mango fool

*I was introduced to luscious, creamy fruit fools when I first moved to England. They are rich
puddings, often made with tart green gooseberries. I have adapted this idea using fresh
mangos and yogurt.*

4 cups mango/tropical fruit,
   nonfat, sugar-free yogurt, such
   as apricot/mango
2 ripe mangoes, cubed (about 1
   pound)
8 small mint sprigs

Fold the mango cubes into the yogurt and spoon
into 8 attractive martini glasses or dessert bowls.
Arrange a mint sprig in each glass. Refrigerate
until 15 minutes before needed. Let come to
room temperature before serving.
Makes 8 servings.

Per serving: 104 calories, 5.8 grams protein,
20.3 grams carbohydrate, 0.2 grams fat (0 saturated),
3 milligrams cholesterol, 96 milligrams sodium,
0.6 grams fiber

helpful hints

● *To blanch the beans and
set their color, they need to
be plunged into iced water
after they are drained. Fill a
roasting tin with water and
ice cubes and place near the
sink. As soon as the beans
are drained, plunge them
into the iced water. When
they are cold, drain.*

● *To cube a mango, slice off
each side as close to the
stone as possible. Cut a
1-inch piece from one half.
Remove the skin from the
slice and cut into thin strips
for a garnish. Take the
mango half in your hand,
skin side down. Score the
fruit in a criss-cross pattern
through to the skin. Bend the
skin backwards so that the
cubes pop up. Slice the
cubes away from the skin.
Repeat with the other half.
Score and slice any fruit left
on the stone.*

buffet for
friends

buffet for friends

This meal fits the nutritional guidelines for the Right Carbs phase.

Informal family gatherings, brunch with friends, or "open-house" parties all call for grazing foods that, when placed on a table, invite everyone to help themselves. This party needs very little attention during the festivities, leaving you to join in the fun.

Menu

Shrimp in Lime-Mustard Sauce
Roasted Meat Platter with Horseradish and Honey Mustard Dressing
Tomato Platter
Pasta Salad
Frozen Yogurt Berry Cup

Countdown

Two days ahead

● Shop for ingredients.

One day ahead

● Arrange meat platter, wrap, and refrigerate.
● Make sauces for meats. Cover and refrigerate.
● Make sauce for shrimp.
● Poach shrimp. Cover and refrigerate.

Morning of the party

● *Arrange shrimp on serving platter, wrap, and refrigerate.*
● *Measure frozen yogurt and place in dessert bowls. Place in freezer. Sprinkle berries around yogurt just before serving.*
● *Slice tomatoes and assemble tomato platter.*
● *Make pasta salad.*

One hour before guests arrive

● *Remove shrimp, meat, and sauces from refrigerator and set on buffet table. Place shrimp sauce near shrimp and meat sauces near meat platter. Drizzle tomatoes with Honey Mustard Dressing. Place bread for meat platter in basket.*
● *Remove yogurt bowls from freezer and sprinkle with berries 15 minutes before serving dessert.*

shopping list

Buy 2 days ahead of party

FRUIT AND VEG

2 limes

1/2 head red-leaf lettuce

1 bunch chives

1 bunch watercress

2 large red tomatoes

2 large yellow tomatoes

2 lemons

1 bunch dill

5 ounces broccoli florets

1 medium cucumber

2 medium red peppers

2 1/2 pounds fresh raspberries

DAIRY

1 carton nonfat plain yogurt
   (10 ounces needed)

DELI

3/4 pound sliced lean deli roast
   beef

3/4 pound sliced roast turkey
   breast

3/4 pound lean sliced ham (no
   honey-baked or glazed)

SEAFOOD

1 1/2 pounds shrimp, peeled
   and deveined

GROCERY

1 bottle horseradish

1 jar honey-flavored mustard

1/2 pound whole wheat penne
   or other whole wheat shortcut pasta

1 carton low-fat, frozen
   strawberry yogurt (32
   ounces needed)

2 packages thin-sliced rye
   bread (32 slices needed)

STAPLES

Mayonnaise

Dijon mustard

Reduced-fat mayonnaise

Salt

Black peppercorns

shrimp in lime-mustard sauce

1¹/₂ pounds shrimp, cooked, peeled, and deveined
6 tablespoons mayonnaise
2 teaspoons Dijon mustard
1¹/₂ tablespoons lime juice

Arrange shrimp in a circle, tails pointed out, on a serving platter. Mix mayonnaise, mustard, and lime juice together in a small bowl. Place the bowl in the center of the platter.
Makes 8 servings.

Per serving: 148 calories, 3.8 grams protein, 26.3 grams carbohydrate, 3.5 grams fat (0.5 saturated), 0 milligrams cholesterol, 0 milligrams sodium, 1.5 grams fiber

helpful hints

● *Shelled shrimp are available at most supermarket seafood counters. The slightly higher cost is worth the time saved.*

● *If you're pressed for time, buy ready-cooked shrimp from the seafood department of the supermarket.*

● *You can substitute lemon juice for the lime juice*

roasted meat platter with horseradish and honey mustard dressing

$^{1}/_{2}$ head red-leaf lettuce

$^{3}/_{4}$ pound sliced lean deli roast beef

$^{3}/_{4}$ pound sliced roast turkey breast

$^{3}/_{4}$ pound lean sliced ham (no honey-baked or glazed)

$^{1}/_{4}$ cup reduced-fat mayonnaise

$1^{1}/_{4}$ cups nonfat plain yogurt

$1^{1}/_{2}$ tablespoons horseradish

$^{1}/_{4}$ cup snipped chives

$1^{1}/_{2}$ tablespoons honey-flavored mustard

32 slices thin-sliced rye bread (or 16 slices medium-sliced rye bread)

To prepare the meat platter, line a serving platter with lettuce leaves. Place meat in radiating rows from the center of the platter to the edge, folding the slices in half and overlapping them. The folded edge should show.

To prepare the horseradish sauce, mix the mayonnaise, $^{1}/_{2}$ cup yogurt, horseradish, and chives together and place in a small bowl. Serve with meat platter.

To prepare the Honey Mustard Dressing, mix the remaining yogurt and honey-flavored mustard together and place in a small bowl. Serve with the meat platter.

Place bread in a basket near the meat for people to make their own sandwiches.

Makes 8 servings.

Per serving: 453 calories, 39.1 grams protein, 43.8 grams carbohydrate, 12.3 grams fat (2.9 saturated), 87 milligrams cholesterol, 1091 milligrams sodium, 2.1 grams fiber

tomato platter

2 large red tomatoes

2 large yellow tomatoes

1–2 tablespoons Honey Mustard
  Dressing from the Roasted
  Meat Platter

1 bunch watercress, for garnish

Slice tomatoes and alternate slices on a serving platter. Drizzle 1–2 tablespoons Honey Mustard Sauce over. Place sprigs of watercress on the side for a garnish.

Makes 8 servings.

Per serving: 46 calories, 2.4 grams protein, 7.6 grams carbohydrate, 0.4 grams fat (0 saturated), 1.0 milligrams cholesterol, 29 milligrams sodium, 0 grams fiber

pasta salad

1/4 cup reduced-fat mayonnaise

2 tablespoons freshly squeezed
    lemon juice

1/4 cup snipped fresh dill

1³/4 cups uncooked whole wheat
    penne or other whole wheat
    short-cut pasta

2 cups small broccoli florets

1 medium cucumber, peeled,
    seeded, and cubed

2 medium red bell peppers, cubed

Salt and freshly ground black
    pepper to taste

Place a large saucepan with 2–3 quarts water to boil. Mix mayonnaise, lemon juice, and dill together in a large serving bowl. Add pasta to boiling water and cook for 5 minutes. Add broccoli and continue to cook for 4 minutes or until pasta is cooked but still firm. Drain and add to serving bowl. Add cucumber, red bell pepper, and salt and pepper to taste.

Makes 8 servings.

Per serving: 123 calories, 4.7 grams protein, 21.4 grams carbohydrate, 3.0 grams fat (0.6 saturated), 3 milligrams cholesterol, 66 milligrams sodium, 3.3 grams fiber

Buffet for Friends p186–93

frozen yogurt berry cup

4 cups low-fat, frozen strawberry
  yogurt
4 cups fresh raspberries

Spoon yogurt into 8 dessert bowls and sprinkle
berries on top.
Makes 8 servings.

Per serving: 151 calories, 3.6 grams protein,
27.1 grams carbohydrate, 3.4 grams fat
(1.5 saturated), 10 milligrams cholesterol,
80 milligrams sodium, 2.9 grams fiber

helpful hints

● *Any fresh berries can be used.*

● *The frozen yogurt can be spooned into dessert bowls and placed in the freezer in the morning. They only need to be removed and sprinkled with berries just before serving. They will also hold for about 30 minutes out of the freezer this way.*

barbecue
party

barbecue party

The meal fits the nutritional guidelines for the Right Carbs phase.

"Let's have a barbecue" is an invitation that brings smiles to everyone. Grilled food is popular year-round and the idea of cooking outside brings sunny thoughts to most of us, even in the winter months.

Most barbecued foods are coated with sugary sauces that have a lot of carbs. This simple barbecue party captures the flavors of the grill without the carbohydrates.

It's easiest to serve this meal buffet-style.

Menu

Spicy Tuna Spread

No-Fuss Salad Bar

Lime Barbecued Chicken with Black Bean Sauce

Green Bean and Orzo Salad

Melon with Marinated Strawberries

Countdown

Two days ahead

- Shop for ingredients.

One day ahead

- Make Spicy Tuna Spread.

- Make black bean sauce for chicken. Cover and refrigerate.
- Prepare and blanch onion and red bell pepper for chicken recipe. Cover and refrigerate.
- Make strawberry sauce and place in a bowl. Cover and refrigerate.

Morning of the party

- Place ingredients for salad bar in attractive bowls. Cover and refrigerate.
- Make Green Bean and Orzo Salad. Wrap and refrigerate.
- Cut melon into slices and place in bowl. Cover and refrigerate.
- Cut cucumber slices for tuna spread. Wrap and refrigerate.

One hour before guests arrive

- Marinate chicken, covered, in refrigerator.
- Light barbecue, if using charcoal.
- Remove tuna spread, black bean sauce, red bell pepper, and onion, orzo salad, and strawberry sauce from the refrigerator.
- Arrange melon on individual dessert plates. Cover with plastic wrap and set aside.
- Set up salad bar on buffet table.

shopping list

Buy 2 days ahead of party

FRUIT AND VEG
  1 bunch basil leaves
  1 small bunch parsley
  1 small bunch cilantro
  2 medium cucumbers
  *2 bags washed, ready-to-
      eat lettuce*
  *1 bag shredded, washed,
      ready-to-eat carrots*
  *2 bags shredded, washed,
      ready-to-eat red
      cabbage*
  *2 bags washed, ready-to-
      eat celery sticks*
  2 red bell peppers
  *2 pounds fresh green
      beans*
  *2½ pounds cherry
      tomatoes*
  3 limes
  2 lemons
  1 honeydew melon
  *2½ pounds fresh
      strawberries*
DAIRY
  *1 small piece Parmesan
      cheese (1 ounce
      needed for Parmesan
      curls)*
MEAT
  *8 x (6-ounce) boneless
      skinless chicken breasts*

Fifteen minutes before guests arrive

● *Place black bean sauce in a saucepan over low heat to heat through.*

● *Spread tuna on cucumber slices and place on serving platter.*

● *Pre-heat gas barbecue.*

● *While guests are having drinks and hors d'oeuvres, grill chicken and place on platter in low oven to keep warm.*

To serve meal

● *Spoon half the black bean sauce on to a serving platter, place chicken on top, and sprinkle with blanched onion and red bell pepper. Serve the remaining sauce in a bowl next to the chicken platter. Place on buffet table.*

● *Place orzo salad on buffet table.*

To serve dessert

● *Pre-heat oven and place biscuits in oven while main dishes are being cleared.*

● *Spoon strawberry sauce over melon and place biscuits on side.*

spicy tuna spread

8 pitted green or black olives

1 (6-ounce) can tuna packed in
   water

2 tablespoons mayonnaise

3 tablespoons horseradish

¼ cup fresh basil leaves, washed
   and dried

2 medium cucumbers, peeled and
   sliced on the diagonal

Place olives, tuna, mayonnaise, horseradish, and basil in a food processor and process until smooth. Taste for seasoning, adding more horseradish if necessary. Just before serving, spread on cucumber slices, and place on serving platter.

Makes 8 servings.

Per serving: 49 calories, 6.3 grams protein, 3.8 grams carbohydrate, 1.3 grams fat (0.1 saturated), 9 milligrams cholesterol, 199 milligrams sodium, 0.6 grams fiber

shopping list(cont)

GROCERY

1 small container pitted green
   or black olives
   (8 olives needed)

1 small jar horseradish

1 small package orzo

1 small container orange juice

1 small package icing sugar

1 package almond-flavored or
   other biscuits

STAPLES

1 (6-ounce) can tuna packed
   in water

Red onion

Garlic

Cayenne pepper

Mayonnaise

No-sugar-added salad
   dressings

Canned black beans
   (16 ounces needed)

Olive oil

Balsamic vinegar

Salt

Black peppercorns

no-fuss salad bar

A colorful salad bar makes a pretty display and is easy to assemble. Here are some tips on how you can put one together without any washing or cutting. Buy a selection of these items from your supermarket: pre-washed lettuce, grated carrots, sliced red cabbage, celery sticks.

2 bags washed, ready-to-eat lettuce
1 cup shredded carrots
2 bags shredded red cabbage
4 cups celery sticks
4 cups cherry tomatoes
8 tablespoons no-sugar-added salad dressing

All you need to do is open the bags and place the vegetables in attractive bowls. Add a bowl of rinsed cherry tomatoes. I have given you guidelines, but you can choose whatever vegetables you like. The secret is to make a colorful display. I like to use different sizes and shapes of bowls for the vegetables and dressing.

For a party it's nice to fill bowls with the dressings. For nutritional values, plan for 1 tablespoon dressing per person.

Buy 2 different types of dressings. Look for dressings that have no sugar added and are made with olive or canola oil.

Per serving: 201 calories, 15G protein, 12G carbohydrate, 11G fat (3G saturated), 426MG cholestorol, 511MG sodium, 3G fiber

lime-barbecued chicken with black bean sauce

1/2 cup fresh lime juice

1 cup olive oil

1 teaspoon cayenne pepper

4 garlic cloves, crushed

8 x (6-ounce) boneless, skinless chicken breasts

1/4 cup chopped red onion

2 red bell peppers, diced

1/4 cup balsamic vinegar

1/2 cup orange juice

2 cups drained and rinsed cooked canned black beans

Salt and freshly ground black pepper

Several sprigs fresh cilantro or parsley, for garnish

To prepare the chicken, mix lime juice, oil, cayenne pepper, and 2 cloves crushed garlic together and pour into plastic bag or bowl. Add the chicken breasts and marinate overnight or about 8 hours. Remove from refrigerator, drain, and bring to room temperature. Seal the juices in the chicken by browning each piece on both sides, about 2 minutes per side. Move chicken to a cooler area of barbecue to finish cooking without burning, about 5 minutes.

To prepare for Black Bean Sauce, mix vinegar, orange juice, remaining 2 cloves garlic, and black beans together and purée in a blender or food processor. Add salt and pepper to taste. Warm in a microwave or in a saucepan. To blanch the onion and red bell pepper, bring a pot of water to the boil and add the onion and red bell pepper. As soon as the water returns to the boil, drain, and rinse under cold water. Or place in a microwave-safe bowl and microwave on high for 3 minutes.

To serve, spoon a little Black Bean Sauce on a serving platter and place the chicken over the sauce. Sprinkle the top with the onion and red bell pepper. Garnish the platter with cilantro or parsley. Serve the remaining sauce on the side. *Makes 2 servings*.

Per serving: 353 calories, 54.0 grams protein, 15.2 grams carbohydrate, 9.3 grams fat (1.9 saturated), 132 milligrams cholesterol, 117 milligrams sodium, 1.8 grams fiber

helpful hints

● *Make sure the grill bars on your barbecue are clean. Spray with vegetable oil spray. If using charcoal, heat the barbecue for about 45 minutes before use or 15 minutes if using gas. The coals should be glowing and the bars hot.*

● *If you do not have a barbecue, then brown the chicken in a very hot sauté pan.*

● *An easy way to marinate the chicken is to place it and the marinade in a self-seal plastic bag. It takes up less space in the refrigerator than a bowl and can be easily flipped over to make sure all sides of the chicken are marinated.*

green bean and orzo salad

1⅓ cups orzo

2 pounds fresh green beans, trimmed and cut into 1-inch pieces

¼ cup olive oil and vinegar dressing

Salt and freshly ground black pepper

1 ounce Parmesan cheese

Bring a large saucepan with 3–4 quarts of water to the boil over high heat. Add the orzo and boil for 5 minutes. Add the beans and continue to boil for 5 minutes more. Drain. Place in a serving bowl and drizzle the dressing on top and toss well. Add salt and pepper to taste. Make Parmesan curls by thinly slicing the Parmesan with a potato peeler. Place the curls on top of the salad.

Makes 8 servings.

Per serving: 224 calories, 7.2 grams protein, 30.0 grams carbohydrate, 10.1grams fat (2.6 saturated), 3 milligrams cholesterol, 108 milligrams sodium, 3.4 grams fiber

melon with marinated strawberries

1 honeydew melon, sliced
2½ pounds fresh strawberries
¼ cup powdered sugar, sifted
2 tablespoons freshly squeezed
    lemon juice
8 almond-flavored or other bought
    biscuits

Wash, hull, and slice strawberries. Blend in sugar and lemon juice. Leave to marinate for 3–4 hours.

Place 2 slices melon on each dessert plate and spoon strawberry sauce on top. Serve 1 biscuit on the side of each plate.

Makes 8 servings.

Per serving: 126 calories, 2.3 grams protein, 30.2 grams carbohydrate, 1 gram fat (0 saturated), 0 milligrams cholesterol, 16 milligrams sodium, 3.3 grams fiber

index

notes

acknowledgments

This book could not have been written without the patience and help of my husband, Harold. From the minute his cardiologist suggested he adopt a low-carbohydrate lifestyle seven years ago, he has helped me to create and test these recipes. Many thanks and much love.

Once again my assistant, Jackie Murrill, spent hours helping me test the recipes and always with a smile. Thank you, Jackie, for your friendship and help.

Lisa Ekus has been my trusted friend for many years and as my agent was a wonderful help in bringing my ideas to the page. Many thanks, Lisa.

I'd also like to thank my family who have always supported my projects and encouraged me every step of the way: my son James, his wife, Patty, and their sons, Zachary and Jacob, who helped taste these recipes; my son Charles and his wife, Lori, who tested recipes via e-mail; my son John, his wife, Jill, and their children, Jeffrey and Joanna, who cheered me on; my sister Roberta and brother-in-law Robert who helped to edit my thoughts and words.

Thanks go to Kathy Martin, my editor at the *Miami Herald*, who has been a friend and booster for my columns and books.

Thank you to Joseph Cooper, Radio Manager for WLRN National Public Radio for South Florida, who has helped and encouraged me with my "Food News and Views" segment on his program, *Topical Currents*.

Thank you to my dear friends, Shep and Bernita King, for letting us take over their kitchen for the original cover photograph.

I'd like to thank the many readers who correspond with me from all over the U.S. to say how much they enjoy the recipes and how much better they feel. This kind of encouragement makes the lonely time in front of the computer worthwhile.

Most important, I'd like to thank all of you who read this book and prepare the meals. I hope you enjoy them and reap the benefits as much as I've enjoyed creating the recipes and watching the wonderful results.